I0464478

CORPORATE RECKONING AHEAD

By Gary Brumback

Corporate Reckoning Ahead
Copyright © 2015 by Gary Brumback
All rights reserved.
ISBN-13:978-1515099192

CONTENTS

Preface--5

Part One. The Age of America's Corpocracy:
How Much Longer?--------------------------------------7

Chapter 1. Government Hands Off and Handouts ----9
Chapter 2. Anything Goes---Until----------------------18

Part Two. Corporate Self Reform:
The Turn Up Initiative---------------------------------- 31

Chapter 3. Some Fundamentals-------------------------32
Chapter 4. Getting Ready----------------------------------39
Chapter 5. Changing Governance---------------------45
Chapter 6. Changing Leadership----------------------51
Chapter 7. Changing Board and
Leadership Customs-- 58
Chapter 8. Becoming a Lowerarchy-------------------73
Chapter 9. Cultivating an Uplifting Culture ---------88
Chapter 10. Managing the Whole Performance------103

Part Three. Corporations and Capitalism:
Life Without Them?---116

Chapter 11. Some Alternatives to Corporations------117
Chapter 12. Socially Responsible Capitalism, Not
Socialism---124

Epilogue--137

Appendix A. Some Examples of Corporate
Wrongdoing---138
Appendix B. America's Sadtistics--------------------142

Appendix C. Applying the Principles of Tall Performance Management--143

Notes--166

About the Author---191

PREFACE

Despite their inefficiencies, wrongdoing, and the vagaries of the marketplace, large corporations throughout almost the entire history of America have generally been aided and sometimes kept afloat by government's soft pedaling of corporate wrongdoing and generous handouts. Originally intended to do the public's bidding, corporations quickly coopted government by "marrying" it shortly after the birth of America.

I have called it the "Devil's Marriage." [1] It was not a shotgun wedding. Politicians' palms get greased. Corporations get virtual immunity from accountability for their endless wrongdoing and handouts to prop up and enrich the bottom line.

There has yet to be an incentive or an outside force to compel either partner to get a divorce. But there are rumbling signs the halcyon "Age of the Corpocracy" (i.e., the "marriage") may not endure later in this century.

The book is not intended to be a blanket indictment of people in or associated with the corpocracy. None of us is a saint. Every one of us yields occasionally to temptations and pressures and corporate and public leaders especially encounter more than their share.

Instead, the book is intended to be first a wake-up call to corporate America that her day of reckoning is coming if she stays on course and second a guide for her to change course.

The book is organized into three parts. Part One, with its two chapters, sets the stage for the rest of the book by describing corporate dependence on government and how that dependency leads to corporate wrongdoing of crisis proportions, which in turn will eventually lead to a day of reckoning for corporations if they don't reform themselves.

Part Two is written with the conviction that corporations are not inherently deficient or psychopathic as some claim. [2] Corporations can heal themselves, and, indeed, they must to survive in the long run. The eight chapters show what corporate reforms are needed and how they can be accomplished.

Part Three considers non corporate ways of organizing to meet society's needs and also alternatives to socially irresponsible capitalism.

PART ONE
THE AGE OF AMERICA'S CORPOCRACY

I hope we shall crush in its birth
the aristocracy of our moneyed
corporations which dare already
to challenge our government to
a trial of strength and bid defiance
to the laws of our country.

---Thomas Jefferson

Jefferson and Madison's proposal to limit corporations' political influence and potential for an economic monopoly was withdrawn because the states were already regulating corporations through stringent state charters. They soon were to become meaningless sheets of paper, however, as states raced to lure more corporations. Corporations continued to flex their muscle and buy influence until they had what they wanted, the American Corpocracy.

I call it the "Devil's Marriage" between corporations and government that corrupts both to the core. [1] Like many marriages, one side, the corporate side, is always telling the other side what to do and not to do by greasing the palms of politicians (e.g., over one half billion dollars from all industries for financing the 2012 general election) and lobbying them until they yield (over two billion dollars in lobbying expenses for 2014). [2] Since money talks, corporations get almost on a daily basis favorable regulations and deregulations, favorable judicial verdicts, welfare handouts, impunity from lawlessness, military help in global exploitation, and laissez-faire capitalism.

The two chapters in Part One set the stage for the rest of the book by giving an overview of this halcyon age for corporations, the likelihood of that age coming to an end, and the implications of that happening for corporations.

CHAPTER 1
HANDS OFF AND HANDOUTS

The Corporate Hypocrisy
Government, keep your hands off
But don't stop the handouts

America's corpocracy always favors corporate interests over public interests in the form of government hands off of corporate wrongdoing, and corporate welfare, or handouts to corporations.

These two forms are what I call "badvantages," because they give advantage to bad behavior. The two are not mutually exclusive. Reduced fines, for example, represent both partial hands off corporate wrongdoing in the form of a slap on the wrist and also a handout by saving the corporation money. International trade protections, another example, are by definition hands off policy by government and a hand out from it. And both examples represent wrongdoing by government because both violate the Constitution and/or other laws and at the very least the spirit of the law or moral code.

Government Hands Off Corporate Wrongdoing

Wrongdoing is any behavior that results in some form and level of physical, psychological or financial harm. Some corporate wrongdoing ought to be illegal but has been legalized by the government. Some of the rest is corporate crime that usually is tolerated by the government. All corporate wrongdoing, and any wrongdoing for that matter, is also unethical and harmful in some way and to some degree regardless of the legality of the behavior.

What follows is an overview of the many ways in which government keeps it hands off corporate wrongdoing.

Sham Charters

During the Crown's corpocracy corporations like the brutish British East Indies were chartered by King George. Wanting no more of that, the framers of the Constitution left it up to the states to do the chartering instead of requiring a uniform federal chartering because the states were already regulating corporations through stringent state charters. That decision proved to be a terrible mistake for it eventually led to sham charters. A few states got the idea that by loosening their restrictions they could attract more business, and soon there was a race to the bottom of charter laxity. It wasn't too long before any corporation in any state could get a charter just for the asking and go off and organize and operate as they pleased.

Freed from any restrictions on size and with trust busters nowhere in sight, any corporation can seek to become monolithic and monopolistic. Freed from any expiration deadlines, any corporation can "outlive its own crimes and atrocities" and can wait out more restrictive administrations eventually replaced by more laissez faire ones. [1] Freed from any restrictions on the very nature of its business, a criminally convicted corporation can "disguise itself, run and hide, or reorganize into a whole new entity to stay in business." [2] I guess they could be called "criminal chameleons."

Corporate Personhood

Not prescribing a federal charter in the Constitution was one mistake too many for the Framers to make. But then they did it again by not outlawing in the Constitution constitutional rights for corporations. Corporations aren't even mentioned in the Constitution. Yet today, thanks to the corporatized Supreme Court corporations enjoy the same Constitutional rights and protections as persons do. But have you ever seen a corporation with eyes, nose, tongue, genitals, and the like?

The Supreme Court's preposterous, un-constitutional, un-American, and dangerous ruling in the Citizens' United case (January 21, 2010) for corporate free speech was just the latest in a long string of Constitutional violations the corporatized Court committed in granting corporations other Constitutional rights derived from corporate personhood; namely, the corporation's right to a) due process, b) be free from unreasonable searches, c) a jury trial in a criminal case, d) compensation for government takings, e) be free of double jeopardy, f) jury trial in a civil case, g) commercial speech, h) political speech, i) dissociate with others' speech, j) equal protection, and k) compensation for regulatory takings that aren't available to real people.

Limited Liability

States initially gave their chartered corporations limited liability only if they provided public services, but with the advent of sham charters, any chartered corporation gets limited liability. State legislators in effect have given shareholders, who are the owners of corporations, a moral waiver. It limits owner liability in cases of corporate wrongdoing only to the potential loss of their initial investments and does not extend to potential costs of the damage done by the wrongdoing. Investors are thus free to buy shares in corporations without having to worry about whether increased share value will be gained through corporate wrongdoing and its harmful consequences to individuals, to society at large, or to the environment.

Tort law supposedly allows individuals harmed by willful or negligent corporate actions and products to sue corporations for monetary compensation. But over the years tort liability has been chiseled away by the judicial doctrines of contributory and comparative negligence, the fellow servant rule, and assumption of risk. [3] These doctrines can sometimes enable the corporation to escape liability altogether or to at least blunt it.

More Hands Off

There are many more kinds of government tolerance of corporate wrongdoing: watchdogs that look the other way or are asleep; escape hatches (e.g., legal loopholes, amnesty, and "safe harbors"); non prosecution or insufficient prosecution and punishment (e.g., deferred prosecutions, double disclaimers, plea bargaining, noncriminal alternatives and wrist slapping); and reckless deregulations. An egregious example of immunity from wrongdoing is the defense industry where recidivist wrongdoers continue being awarded lavish government contracts. [4]

Government Handouts to Corporations

The government's dowry to corporate America is a veritable grab bag of handouts that help keep free-loading and inefficient corporations afloat by not adding additional costs to their multiple inefficiencies (see Part Two). They all add up to hundreds of billions of dollars lost yearly for the general welfare promised in the preamble to the Constitution.

Warfare Welfare

War, Albert Einstein once said, is an act of murder. In my recent analysis of war I demonstrated convincingly I believe that it fails to meet 13 "litmus tests" of ever being necessary and just. [5]

That total failure means that the trillion dollar annual federal budget for national security amounts to massive welfare for the defense and intelligence industries.

Just since 1948 over 20 trillion dollars reportedly has been spent on the military budget. [6] I once estimated that one-half of that amount is sheer "warfare welfare," the other half reflecting a realistic defense budget limited to the costs of responding to attacks on our shores by foreign states and terrorist groups. That amounts to at least over 10 trillion dollars in money squandered that could have been spent over more than a 60-year period on meeting pressing domestic and global needs in employment, education, nutrition, health care, sanitation, you name it. [7]

Warfare welfare may be the only big handout initiated by government. But the defense and intelligence industries become so addicted to it that they contrive countless schemes to enlarge it (e.g., reimbursements for cost overruns, contracts awarded to build surplus planes, locating plants in the districts of influential members of Congress, etc., etc.).

Tax Breaks and Other Subsidies

> *I like paying taxes.*
> *It buys me civilization."*
> ---Justice Oliver Wendell Holmes

Corporations are part of civilization, the parasitic part. They depend on civilization but depend on government and the tax paying public to shoulder much of the costs of civilization, including the massive externalization by corporations of such costs as the pollution of common property like air and water.

The think tank, Citizens for Tax Justice, has reported that many American corporations are paying federal income taxes "far below the 35 percent rate often cited as the highest in the world. And many of the most profitable companies are effectively paying no taxes at all." [8]

The Government Accounting Office reported that corporate tax breaks cost the government $180 billion a year. Since GAO is a government entity I imagine it has little incentive to report any higher of a figure. Its estimate presumably accounts for the different versions tax breaks such as tax credits, lowered tax rates, and tax exemptions. The estimate does not include tax deferrals reportedly totaling $1.7 trillion that are kept offshore indefinitely by multinational corporations chartered in the U.S. If corporations had their complete way, a territorial tax system would be created freeing them forever from any U.S. taxes whatsoever. [9]

Tax breaks are one form of government subsidies. The others include direct subsidies like cash grants and interest-free loans and indirect subsidies like insurance coverage, low-interest loans, depreciation write-offs, and rent rebates. The Cato Institute has estimated that direct federal subsidies to corporations, for example, costs taxpayers almost $100 billion every year. [10] One positive feature of government subsidies is when they are used to compensate a corporation for entering an unprofitable but socially needed market.

State governments are not stingy either in giving non-tax subsidies. The New York Times has reported for instance that 48 companies "received more than $100 million in state grants since 2007. Some 5,000 other companies have received more than $1 million in recent years. General Motors, for instance, was awarded at least $1.77 billion since 2007 from 208 grants in 16 states. [11]

Bailouts

When I was doing the research for The Devil's Marriage book, what I call Economic Katrina began howling through Main Street and Wall Street. It became the second largest depression since the Great Depression. Main Street went under. Wall Street and big corporations did not. Authorized to do so by the Emergency Economic Stabilization Act passed by Congress in 2008 the Treasury Department handed out over $600 billion in rescue money to the banking industry, the mortgage industry, the insurance industry, the automotive industry, and other industries. [12] While it is true that some of the money has been paid back to government, the public will ultimately end up in the red.

Bail outs, more so than all of the other forms of corporate welfare, reveal how inept corporations really are at doing business and how a "too big to fail" mentality has been engrained among them.

The Chrysler Corporation is a good example of corporate dependency on government. The company has been bailed out twice in recent history at a tremendous cost to the government and thus to the public. Yes, the bailed out automaker responded by building popular minivans, but a recent study suggests that the company could have fared

better in the long run without these bailouts if it had made some changes in the way it did business. [13]
Privatization

If corporate America and her ideological cheerleaders had their way all public service would become private service. Very few public services have escaped some degree and form of privatization and the holdouts such as Social Security are being eyed covetously by the private sector. Even corporations seemingly far afield from the kinds of services privatized have gotten into the act.

The world's largest defense contractor, Lockheed Martin, for example, besides making and selling deadly weapons, sorts the mail but is not the USPS; cuts Social Security checks but is not the SSA; counts the census but is not the Bureau of the Census; monitors air traffic; but is not the FAA; runs space flights but is not NASA; and helps spy on Americans but is not NSA. [14]

Privatization is a big government handout because corporations profit considerably with little initial investment.

Free Trade Agreements

The first adjective says it all, "free," as in "corporate freedom to operate globally without any government constraints. These agreements represent not only a government hands-off policy but also amount to a huge give away, the globe's resources for the taking by powerful multinational corporations. Over 3,000 of them are headquartered in the U.S., and the foreign assets of some of these corporations account for more than half of their total assets. [15]

16

More Handouts

Other types of government handouts to corporations include debt forgiveness, discounted insurance, excessive payments to contractors, giving away public resources, loan guarantees, price support loans, quotas, and R & D funding.

Overall, corporate welfare amounts to more than $100 billion yearly in handouts to corporations and dwarfs social welfare. Government is a Robin Hood in reverse, taking from the poor (e.g., reducing food stamp benefits) and giving to wealthy corporations.

Summary

Corporations are making out like bandits from all the government handouts and, as the next chapter shows, are acting like bandits from all the government hands offs.

CHAPTER 2
ANYTHING GOES---UNTIL

Ted Nace, author, consultant, and founder of a publishing company, called them "gangs of America." [1] He wasn't referring to hoodlums in the "hood." He was referring to corporations. With no moral compass, their eyes on their bottom line and easy money for the taking with impunity, corporations are recidivist wrongdoers day in and day out.

In Appendix A are some examples of corporate wrongdoing. Much of it is has been made perfectly legal by government. What is illegal government allows or penalizes superficially. All of it is perfectly unethical, violating one or more of these universal moral values: accountability, caring for and respecting others, excellence, fairness, honesty, integrity, loyalty, promise keeping, justice, and responsibility. [2] And all of it is harmful to varying degrees and kinds.

Outliers and Bona Fide Ethical Corporations?

Appendix A is not intended to be a broad brush indictment of all corporations. There are thousands of them, from behemoth to small so one would think any search ought to find some outliers (i.e., less corruptible corporations) and a few truly ethical corporations. Some searchers, though, have ended up with egg on their faces, as in the case of the pundits who touted Enron before its colossal fall and afterwards found themselves unflatteringly depicted in Business Week. [3]

Or like the now defunct Business Ethics journal that published its five-year list of "best corporate citizens." At the top of it was Fannie May, charged at about the same time by the SEC of having violated its rules for years, and Fannie Mae was not the only undeserving company on the list. [4]

Or, like GE that kept emerging as "the most admired company," yet "has a long history of unethical and illegal practices."[5] This corporation was more recently touted by a pair of academic researchers as being socially responsible, yet in my published commentary on their assertion I pointed out that it is among the top five polluters; unmatched in the number of jobs outsourced and plants closed; a heavy hitter in political campaign contributions; a "top spender" in lobbying; a moocher of over three quarter of a billion dollars in government grants just for the year 2012; a tax avoider; and a major defense contractor. [6]

I once tried my own search and failed. I had read over 100 reports from several years of websites of corporations that had been identified as financially successful for a long time. To the extent that the reports are valid (websites are hardly foolproof sources of information), it seems that all but one of the companies may have been cutting ethical corners at least occasionally while doing business and may sometimes have also run afoul of the law. One of the cases even spiraled up to the US Supreme Court, which barely overturned an appellate court decision in favor of the plaintiff rather than the corporation. [7]

Controlling Our Life Equations

You, me, everyone has the same general equation to express our lives. It may just be the most important non-mathematical equation anyone will ever see in their lifetime:

$$\text{Our Selves} + \text{Our Situations} = \text{Whether/How Much}$$
$$\text{Health, Happiness, and Prosperity}$$
$$\text{We Have or Don't Have}$$

"Life, liberty, and the pursuit of happiness" are more than "just" declarations of the sanctity and importance of our life's equations. It's an affirmation of humanity and support for the general welfare in a civilized society.

Most Americans do not control their own lives. Corporate America and its partner in crime Government America do. The life equations for all but the wealthiest Americans look like this:

$$\text{Our Selves} + \text{The Corpocracy} = \text{Much, Much Less}$$
$$\text{Health, Happiness, and Prosperity}$$

Most Americans in the eyes and minds of the corpocracy are like commodities to be treated no differently from inanimate things that can be acquired, used, and traded or trashed. Most Americans will never have an opportunity to be fully human. That is no exaggeration when you consider all of the unfulfilled human needs in America.

And just what are humanity's needs? I believe the late psychologist Abraham Maslow knew the answer after all the research and thinking he did on the question. [8] There are five human needs according to Maslow, arranged in a hierarchy with the lower "rung" needs having priority over the others. The first rung is the physiological need to fill one's belly and to sleep protected under a roof. The next three are the needs to be safe, to be loved and belong, and to have self-esteem. If those four needs are all being fulfilled, there is only one left to be fulfilled. He called it "self-actualization," or reaching one's fullest potential and becoming the most of what one can become.

Corporate America along with Government America is keeping Americans who struggle daily to make ends meet at the lowest levels and most of the remaining Americans from ever reaching their fullest potential. The corpocracy clearly is malevolent, not benevolent.

Really Serious Consequences

The foregoing discussion of Maslow's hierarchy of needs, my concept of life's equations, and the rest of Appendix A are rather abstract, very general, and encompass all of America's industries. Now let's take a brief look at some industries in which the consequences of corporate wrongdoing can be serious to say the least. The corporations involved are mostly the larger ones.

The War Industry

Does Einstein's opinion that war "is an act of murder" mean that any maker of murderous weaponry is a surrogate murderer? Whatever war means to you and whether you think it is ever just and necessary, war is a trillion dollar business with millions of casualties over the years and counting. Are domestic arms makers any different from weapons makers given the gun homicides in America of nearly epidemic proportions?

The Spy Industry

America was born with a musket in one hand and a spy glass in the other. Warrior-in-chief George Washington valued secrecy and spying on the enemy. Today, there are hundreds of corporations in the spy industry imperiling the right to privacy of U.S. citizens by supplying government with equipment for spying not only on the enemy but also on the U.S. citizenry, collecting through various spy medium (e.g., using small aircraft to trick cell phones to reveal messages) mountains of data on the public and storing the data in a huge and ridiculously costly citizens' "metadata" store house in Utah.

The Chemical and Agricultural Industry

I put the chemical and agribusiness industries together because the latter uses the former in saturating our food chain. There's an old nostrum that "we are what we eat," which is why this industry is so hazardous and sometimes deadly, especially with their widespread use of herbicides and genetically modified organisms, or GMOs. There is a growing and alarming record of illnesses and deaths associated with the use of herbicides. [9] And with the proliferation of GMOs in our food chain the industry is "playing with genetic fire" concludes the medical director of the Natural Foods Foundation. [10] Anything goes with this industry as they have the Food and Drug Administration and the rest of government in their pocket.

The Pharmaceutical Industry

What's in our medicine cabinets? Americans should never take for granted the safety, appropriateness, and cost of any prescribed medications. If Americans only knew how unsafe and deadly drugs may be, how unscrupulously new drugs are developed and tested and get approved by the U.S. Food and Drug Administration (FDA), are promoted, are priced and marketed, how unscrupulous big pharma can be in other ways, and how government is captured by big pharma. [11] On that last point, Big Pharma is second to none in lobbying Congress and gets a whopping 77,500% return on its "investment." [12]

The unexpected and/or untold possible adverse reactions from taking "bad pills" prescribed for various ailments can be horrifying. There are reportedly over 100,000 deaths a year, and 2.1 million serious injuries from adverse drug reactions. [13] As a recent heart attack victim, when I reach into my medicine cabinet I trust the prescribed drugs I am taking will continue to be life extending, not ending.

The Energy Industry

Are our water and milk safe to drink? More than half of the nation's drinking water from underground aquifers is being poisoned by energy and mining companies allowed by government to do so. [14] The largely unregulated nuclear power sector of this industry with its aging reactors is particularly worrisome given the Fukushima disaster and with radioactive isotopes being detected in our children's milk. [15]

Is our air safe to breathe? In this industry are almost one-half of the top 100 corporate air polluters. [16] There are more than half a dozen air pollutants we breathe that have both acute and chronic effects on our health, including "premature mortality and reduced life expectancy." [17]

Answers to those two questions depend partly and for the time being on where one lives and how well off one is. That is less true, depending on whether one is a "climate denier," with global warming and its adverse effects. Climate affects everyone to some degree and in various ways. This industry is largely responsible for the climate crisis with its melting ice caps blistering temperatures and the like that has no geographic boundaries. [18]
Species other than our own answer those questions in their own ways. For some species their answer is their extinction. According to the Center for Biological Diversity

dozens of species become extinct every day. [19]. And more than a million species of animals and plants risk extinction just this century due to human activity, no small part of it by this industry. According to one university ecologist, "Loss of biological diversity due to species extinctions is going to have major impacts on our planet---. [20]

Just think for a moment about what is happening to what. Air, water, animal and plant species are what Nature is giving to us at no cost other than to protect them, not harm and destroy them. In terms of total and irreversible harm it does to all species and their environment, this industry may be second only to the war industry.

The Transportation Industry

The scale of the life and death consequences of wrongdoing by this industry pales in comparison to the industries just sketched. Nevertheless, it is included here because it has a long track record of wrongdoing, starting at least as early as the 1940s when six corporations from this industry and the energy industry conspired to rid municipalities of their trolley lines to "pave" the way for buses. [21]

The industry's record was tracked throughout the 1990s and showed eight of its corporations on the list of top 100 corporate criminals. [22] More recently, an insider has called the trucking sector the most corrupt in the industry, [23] and an expert on corporate compliance has called the shipping sector the most corrupt of all industries. [24]

The auto makers' sector of this industry probably will never forget Unsafe at Any Speed that catapulted its author, Ralph Nader, onto the public stage in the mid60s. [25] More than half a century later one of the corporations featured in his book has appeared in the news about a scandal "involving corporate malfeasance, regulatory ineptitude, and at least thirteen deaths." [26]

The Financial Services Industry

It is well that the people
of the nation do not
understand our banking
and monetary system,
for if they did, I believe
there would be a revolution
before tomorrow morning.
--Henry Ford [27]

All wars are bankers' wars!
---Michael Rivero [28]

When it comes to financing military and drug wars (including drug money laundering), trading in unregulated and risky securities, foreclosing on homes banks duped them into buying, and the like this industry ought to be called the financial "disservices" industry. It was clearly responsible for the Second Great Depression to hit America, this time in 2008. Main Street was swept away. Wall Street was kept high and dry by its government partner

The Mass Media

One of the greatest heists of the American people was when government turned over the free public airwaves to corporate America. Today, a handful of large corporations own the mass media of see and tell; that is, see and tell what the corporations and their government sponsors want us to see and know. This industry, in concert with the Bush

25

administration, sold the general public (the masses who are easily fooled) the Iraq WMDs and ensuing war hook, line, and sinker awash in a bloodbath of innocents. I don't think it's an exaggeration to say that the mass media has mas blood on its hands indirectly and that the U.S. could not get by with its endless warring and spying without the mass media.

This industry is also no slacker when it comes to promoting the baubles, bangle, and beads Americans are persuaded to want and buy.

Until
The Days of Reckoning

The harm done by the industries sketched, when added to all of the harm done by the rest of the some 16 industries with government as either an accomplice, or a direct agent in the case of warring and spying, is directly responsible for the list of "sadstistics" in Appendix B that reflect the nation's current, dismal conditions. [29] America has become a third world country (e.g., America's ranks worst among so-called advance nations on some of the conditions), a terrorist nation (the majority of people polled around the world regard America as the greatest threat to world peace), a failed nation by not even living up to the minimal requirements of its Constitution, and a nation in which most of its citizenry never get the opportunity to fulfill all of their human needs, and in that sense are only part human. [30]

So much misery, death and environmental harm inflicted by America's corpocracy on Americans and on the rest of the world are bound to produce "boomerang harm." It can arrive in a variety of forms, from different origins, with varying intensity, with varying scope, with varying onsets, with varying effects, and with varying duration and finality. Some have already started appearing.

Grave and Irreversible

Genocide
Ecocide
Nuclear Attacks
Armageddon

The final reckoning for humanity, whether it be its wrongdoers, accomplices, passive bystanders, and everyone else would be Armageddon. It may someday be a reality, not just a scriptural prophecy. Humanity has had the capacity for total self-destruction ever since America introduced nuclear bombs to the world.

Since then nine countries thereabout currently possess nuclear weapons. [31] Not all of them have signed a treaty agreeing to discontinue expanding their nuclear weapon capability. The U.S. has the most adversarial relations with three of those nations, China, North Korean, and Russia. Sometimes the disputes become overheated and high-level warnings by one or both parties are issued. Whether these verbal exchanges would ever culminate in an exchange of nuclear bombs hurling back and forth remains to be seen. Some pundits argue that U.S. militarism is heading us toward WWIII. [32] If so, it would more than likely include nuclear attacks.

Violence from the Inside

Revolution
Sporadic and Localized Uprisings

America was born in the womb of war, the American Revolution. That one wasn't enough to suit Thomas Jefferson, apparently, for he once said "Every generation needs a new revolution." That probably has never been uttered since by any of his successors. They have gradually turned the nation into a fortress to stem even a hint of a revolution.

There have been, of course, sporadic and violent uprisings in the history of America that have been quelled by her regimes. Four that that come to mind are Shay's rebellion in 1786-87, the aftermath of the Rev. Martin Luther King Jr.'s assassination, the Vietnam War protest, and the radical underground of the 70's. Recently there has been a spate of localized uprisings over injustice and police brutality.

Violence from Outside

Episodic Blowbacks
Escalating and Serial Blowbacks

Blowback is an exercise in retributive justice, an eye for an eye. Internal uprisings are one form of blowback. The other involves actions against a nation by sources outside of it. By "escalating blowbacks" I mean repeated retaliations against the same target(s) that increase in size, intensity, and harm done. Escalating blowbacks lead to a "mass of bodies for a mass of bodies."

The deadly "9/11" al-Qaeda terrorist air strikes were heinous, punishable acts, no doubt about it, but they were also blowback by people seeking to settle a score for America's skewed foreign policy, imperialism, heavy military presence, and covert and overt deadly interventions in the Greater Middle East.

28

America's military aggressions in over 130 countries [33] create enemies in those countries and in the opinion of several high-level government insiders and also knowledgeable outsiders like Ralph Nader figuratively invite those enemies to retaliate. [34]

Non Violent and Imposed

Movements
Demonstrations/Protests
Boycotts
Petitions
Legal Challenges
Ballot Box Choices

The majority of Americans believe both corporations and government are too big and powerful. Countless Americans, furthermore, have specific grievances about the harm experienced from the corpocracy's wrongdoing and join usually issue-specific demonstrations, protests and larger-scale movements, all of which have had minimal impact to date. The same can be said about boycotts, petitions, legal challenges, and the ballot box. They are all mostly failed attempts to hold the corpocracy accountable.

But for any sane American resorting to any form of violence to force reforms is not an option. Violence begets violence. Failed non-violent approaches are still useful learning experiences for wronged and discontented Americans. Once they realize the various issues are interconnected if for no other reason than that they have a common origin, America's corpocracy, then corporations and government will be up against formidable, unified opposition and implacable demands for reforms. History shows, Ralph Nader contends with supporting examples (e.g., women's suffrage), that it would take only a dedicated few, or the "other 1%, to gain momentum to enact change. [35]

Self -Imposed Reckoning

Voluntary Government Reforms
Voluntary Corporate Reforms

Government will not reform itself. It is indebted to and controlled by corporate America and impassioned ideologues promoting American hegemony and using militarism to achieve it.

In the halcyon age of America's corpocracy its corporations have never had an incentive to reform themselves---until. Until they realize their eventual survival depends on it, the subject of Part Three.

Summary

America's corporations long ago learned how to milk and manipulate America's governments at all levels and branches, have enriched themselves by operating as if anything goes, have mostly avoided any substantive accountability for their massive wrongdoing---until. There are abundant signs that the halcyon era of the American corpocracy may be slowly coming to an end through one or more forms of externally imposed reckonings. Government will not reform itself. To survive corporations must reform themselves, and in the process government will follow suit.

PART TWO
CORPORATE SELF REFORM
THE TURN UP INITIATIVE

You never change things by
fighting the existing reality.
To change something, build
a new model that makes the
existing model obsolete.
　　　　---R. Buckminster Fuller

In my two most recent books I built a new model to replace the corpocracy and end America's endless warring and spying. I called it "Alter America." [1]

In Part Two of this book, I present my model of a totally rebuilt corporation based on my 50 some years of research and writing as an organizational psychologist. The model presented here is a short version of a very detailed version presented in two of my other books. [2]

While I know of no corporation that looks and acts exactly like the model corporation, I do know of a few corporations with some features like or similar to some of the model's features.

Part Two is for four audiences: the general public to show it what is possible; people who study, write about corporations and organizations in genera and teach and consult; influential and enlightened people in corporations; and diehard members of the corpocracy who will turn their backs on the book but just maybe have second thoughts.

CHAPTER 3
SOME FUNDAMENTALS

What Corporate Turn Up Is Not

First, it is not a corporate turnaround. Most turn around initiatives rarely meet expectations and some end disastrously as in the extreme case of Al Dunlap, one of the most publicized turn around "artists" of the 1990's. He sent Sunbeam into a tailspin, was fired, and agreed to settle the SEC charges that he defrauded Sunbeam and to be barred from holding executive positions in public companies. [1]

A turnaround artist would be ill-equipped to conceive and lead a corporate turn up aimed at raising performance to new heights. The two initiatives are very different conceptually. A turnaround really has no conceptual framework for understanding and guiding an organizational transformation. A turnaround also has an unfortunate connotation, going in circles or reversing course. A turn up in contrast requires a fresh new paradigm for thinking about fundamental concepts like the full meaning of tall performance, the finer differentiations of success and failure, and many other important matters. A turn up, moreover, connotes precisely the right direction performance needs to take, upwards.

The two are very different operationally. The turn up initiative goes far beyond a typical turnaround effort. The latter at best usually amounts to rescue efforts. A distressed company calls upon a turn-around specialist or a new CEO to come in and basically do a quick fix on one or more trouble spots. At worst, the company goes into a tailspin and crashes.

Corporate turn up is not corporate restructuring. "Few phrases," the financial columnist James Surowieck begins, "are duller than 'corporate restructuring,'" and then goes on to mention as a case in point GE's shedding of most of it financial services businesses to concentrate on its industrial businesses. [2] For GE to ever shed the causes of its short performance, as depicted in Chapter 2, would require a major corporate turn up.

A company need not be in some kind of a crisis to launch a turn up, but there are two overriding reasons for doing so. First, as already noted, America's corpocracy, including its corporations is on a collision course with more consequential reckonings. Second, even if the first reason were false, most if not all corporations need to raise their standard of performance and redesign them-selves to reach that standard because it is the right and successful thing to do..

Those two reasons for launching a corporate turn up, however, are unlikely to make it happen. A corporate crisis or a corpocracy-wide crisis (e.g., one or more of the days of reckoning listed in Chapter 2 become more probable and sooner than later) could conceivably make it happen. As they say, necessity is the mother of invention.

What Corporate Turn Up Is

Changing From Short Inputs to Tall Inputs

Short Inputs	Tall Inputs
Speculative Owners	Enduring Owners
Warped Board	Straightened Board
The Wrong CEO	The Right CEO
Hierarchy	Lowerarchy
Short Culture	Tall Culture

Ethics Office	Internalized Ethics
Performance	Performance
Mismanagement	Management
Corpocracy	Democracy

If the new and raised performance standard for the corporation, a standard called here "tall performance," is to be the corporation's beacon and there is consensus that the tall inputs to corporate performance shown are indeed the ones that need to exist in the transformed corporation, then the details of any turn up initiative become less critical as long as the strategy is guided by that beacon. The differences between the short and tall inputs to corporate performance will become clear as we proceed through the rest of Part Two. Take note that one of the inputs, that of the corpocracy vs democracy is both corporate and situational elements. It is also the one over which any corporation by itself has the least overall control.

The inputs listed are not the customary ones that corporations consider and manage. They are capital, labor, and supplies such as raw materials, location, and facilities. This book doesn't deal with them, but they would be dealt with wisely if the corporation changes to the positive inputs on the list.

Turn Up to What?

Tall Performance
Positive Behavior + Positive Results
Not Short Performance
As in
Anything Goes

A Few More Fundamentals

The Performance Equation

Here is the corporate version of the life's equation introduced in the second chapter:

The Corporation + The Corporation's Situations =
Corporate Behavior + Corporate Results

Corporate performance is represented on the output side with two components, corporate behavior, or actions, and the results, or consequences of the behavior.

The two inputs on the left side always interact with each other. Neither one is ever solely responsible for corporate performance. Both the wrong and right inputs for tall performance have already been identified.

An Unconventional Bottom Line

The conventional bottom line of business we all know about, the bottom line of results. The unconventional bottom line, which I call the "bottom line of behavior," is not so familiar. Try to picture it as three-in-one bottom lines, each with positive behavior above the line and negative behavior below it. One line divides competent from incompetent behavior. Another divides motivated from unmotivated behavior. The third divides ethical from unethical behavior. All behavior below any one or more of these lines fall far short of what ought to be expected of any corporation and automatically rules out performing tall regardless of how robust its conventional bottom line might look. Needless to say, the anything goes behavior typical of corporations is not tall performance.

35

Positive results can never be reflected solely in any set of financial measures. Achieving positive results does not require achieving double-digit growth in financial returns every year or maximizing shareholder wealth. Both of these goals are a sure invitation to corporate wrongdoing. Positive results are those that create a positive, multifaceted, and multidirectional value. The value is positive because good benefits have been provided without knowingly causing harm. The value is multifaceted because the benefits aren't just financial ones. And the value is multidirectional because the benefits are not just limited to shareholders and people within the corporation.

Those characteristics of positive results in addition to whatever are the marketplace circumstances need to guide corporate decisions about the production of particular products and services.

Nature of Corporate Success and Failure

One way to think of the conventional and unconventional bottom lines is to think of the difference they make when combined in how success and failure are managed. From the perspective of the first bottom line a success is a success because the desired results are gotten, and a failure is a failure because the desired results are not gotten. All successes are rewarded. All failures are penalized. That's how the notion of success and failure is typically treated in corporations.

Since corporations obviously cannot survive on just their good behavior (nor can Broadway survive on just good acting without enough paying audiences) the practical implications of the unconventional bottom line are mostly in its merger with the conventional one so that the positive and negative dimensions of corporate behavior are taken into account in considering the extent to which corporate goals are met. Adding the two bottom lines together gives a totally different picture of success and failure and allows for the total management and accountability for corporate performance. This merger conveys a truth learned in childhood and often neglected in adulthood. Not all success is good, particularly ill-gotten or negative success, where the ends justify the means. Not all failure is bad or negative, particularly failure where all three kinds of behavior behind it were well above their own respective bottom lines but were thwarted by unfavorable and unforeseen circumstances.

This old truth needs to be revived and made a prevailing creed and practice throughout the corporate world. It is obviously a truth hard to honor in practice. It requires not only the acceptance of positive failures but also the willingness sometimes to reward major risk taking efforts that fail despite plenty of competence, motivation, and integrity that went in to the efforts. While positive failures do not reflect the tallest performance, they can help set the stage for it. Consider, for instance, a company that rewards the members of a project team that spent millions, their talent, and their energy on a worthy gamble that failed due to totally unforeseen circumstances. Such a company wisely knows that the same positive efforts, not being dampened, may very well succeed the next time.

The old truth also requires intolerance of all negative successes and the additional moral courage to penalize the ill-gotten ones, which helps to explain why the old truth is not often seen in action. Consider, for instance, an executive who fires the manager of the leading sales division because he was unscrupulous. Such an executive is more resistant to the conventional bottom line and its pressures and less tempted by its promise of rewards.

Summary

Nothing about a corporation is more crucial to its continued existence than its performance with or without the support of government. As the age of the American corpocracy and anything goes comes to an end nothing will be more important to the corporation than the raising of its short performance to tall performance through choosing and carrying out a corporate turn up initiative that will require a total overhauling of all the corporation's inputs to its performance.

CHAPTER 4
GETTING READY

General Roadmap
for
Launching the Turn Up Initiative

Champion the turn-up initiative.
Convey determination to succeed.
Establish a steering council and task forces.
Remove obstacles before too late.
Arrange for short-term wins.
Launch the Initiative Corporate Wide.

I have drawn this roadmap after reviewing the findings of John Kotter, a Harvard business professor, who watched for over a decade more than 100 large and small companies "try to remake themselves into significantly better competitors" through such efforts as "total quality management, reengineering, right sizing, restructuring, cultural change, and turnaround." [1] Most, Kotter concluded, succeeded only partially or failed completely due to a number of mistakes made: not creating a great enough sense of urgency; not creating a sufficiently powerful coalition to guide the effort; not creating a vision of the firm's future or not broadcasting the vision throughout the firm; not clearing hurdles, such as obstinate managers along the way to the envisioned future; not arranging for short-term wins; and declaring the effort a success prematurely, usually by skipping important stages.

Although Kotter's cases are not completely relevant (apparently none, e.g., involved shortening a hierarchy into a lowerarchy of self-managed teams), there is enough generality to the lessons he drew to consider here.

However, I have made some substantial modifications, the reasons for which will become readily apparent.

Championing the Turn-Up Initiative

The turn-up initiative must be championed by people at the top, not commanded by them. Barking out orders would be in keeping with an ordinary turn-around initiative but totally out of keeping with a turn-up initiative. The CEO will need to explain why the tall inputs are tall and the short inputs are short. The CEO will also need to patiently work through the rest of the road map while building a coalition of allies among members of the corporation and allowing them to mobilize further support, develop momentum, and reach turn-up decisions multilaterally rather than unilaterally.

Conveying Determination to Succeed

A sense of urgency, contrary to Kotter's conclusion, is not what should be created. Urgency is a relative matter, ranging from no crisis to a real crisis existing. Cries of wolf are an unacceptable means of rallying the troops. I was absolutely astonished to see that Kotter approvingly mentions that a "crisis was manufactured in a few of the most successful cases," and gives the example of a CEO who deliberately created "the largest accounting loss in the company's history," which in turn invited strong pressure from Wall Street. [2] This in my opinion is reprehensible behavior that, if it leads to success, can be nothing other than a negative success.

What needs to be conveyed is a sense of determination to walk the talk. An e-mail message to all corporate members needs to be sent from the CEO and endorsed by the board of directors that conveys the determination to succeed and the roadmap to be followed.

Establishing a Steering Council and Task Forces

Kotter concludes from his findings that opposition will eventually mobilize and thwart corporate reform initiatives unless a powerful enough coalition is established to overcome the opposition. His recommendation, though, is the old, stale paradigm of pulling together a large group of senior executives to mount the charge. I can well imagine what the people in the trenches would be thinking in those circumstances; "here we go again, the old guard and establishment reinventing the old guard and establishment." I wonder what would be found if Kotter's companies with their powerful coalitions were visited today.

The new paradigm should instead call for the CEO to create and empower a council to steer implementation of the turn up strategy. The CEO's corporate-wide e-mail message mentioned earlier would go on to invite self-nominations for membership on a representative council empowered to steer implementation of the entire strategy on behalf of the board, the CEO, the corporation, and all its other stakeholders and ask for an indication of openness or receptivity to the strategy. This request might also serve as a not-so subtle alert to the five to 20 percent of the troublemakers and foot draggers who always are around in any large organization.

Membership on the council needs to be representative of all organizational layers but weighted in favor of noteworthy performers. Performance as a qualification must always take priority over rank and seniority. While the backing of the board and CEO are crucially necessary, the ultimate success or failure of the implementation is in the hands of the empowered steering council. That empowerment must be accompanied by competence and commitment. On the other hand, there is something to be said for trying to co-opt the troublemakers and foot draggers. A few of the more influential ones therefore probably should be included on the council and a diplomatic effort made to win them over.

Being fully empowered means that the council would be in charge, is assured the resources necessary for implementation, and defers to the CEO only when the latter has concurrence rights and veto power over "momentous" decisions within the purview of the council. The CEO would predetermine with the board the criteria defining a decision as momentous enough to be outside the council's purview and then tells the council at the outset what the criteria are. They are as narrowly defined as the CEO and board would feel comfortable in defining them.

The council would establish working taskforces responsible for actually implementing each of the major elements of the initiative. There would be at a minimum a taskforce on lowering the hierarchy, on changing the corporate culture, and on managing performance, not mismanaging it.

Removing Obstacles Before Too Late

This prescription, while clearly a no-brainer, is often not taken. Kotter mentions that organizational structure is often an obstacle. Well, that structure is going to be dismantled as the turn-up initiative progresses. He says that compensation or performance appraisal systems sometimes reward the people standing in the way. Well, performance mismanagement is going to be stopped.

But worst of all, he says, are obstinate mid-level managers "who refuse to change and who make demands inconsistent with the overall effort." [3] So among the old guard who has clawed their way up the ladder, some will be resentful, defiant, and intent on sabotaging the initiative. Each will require a tailored response. The worst mistake, though, is not to respond at all, to procrastinate and to let the problem fester.

Arranging for Small Wins

The turn up initiative will probably take several years before the corporation shows consistent progress toward becoming a truly tall performing company, so arranging for short-term wins along the way to thwart discouragement or disillusionment is good advice. Kotter cited examples of companies declaring after two or three years that their reengineering work had succeeded, yet in no less than the same number of years later, little or no trace of the work was evident. More patience is thus advisable.

But only a bit more patience I would caution in light of Kotter's observation that it may take five to ten years for a major transformation to take hold in the organization's culture and become the customary way of being a business and doing the business. That is showing entirely too much patience in my opinion. It is too easy to exaggerate the difficulty of making major and lasting changes successfully. One pair of organizational consultants, for instance, equates a major organizational change with the American Revolution! [4] That is sheer hyperbole in my opinion, and I would be wary of any consultants who came in expressing that opinion.

There is another caveat to keep in mind. The small wins must be meaningful and positive ones, not contrived or negative successes. The first big win will come when the initial phases in changing the inputs have occurred. There will be many more opportunities for interim wins, small and large, along the way to tall performance.

Launching the Initiative Corporate Wide

The turn up initiative should be launched corporate-wide, no matter how large the corporation. Hybrid corporations, part tall, part short, do not work well. Furthermore, pilot testing it only in parts of the corporation is not a good idea. The reasons for putting in place the tall inputs are compelling enough. Pilot tests convey tentativeness and less than full commitmEnt and also allow time for opposition from the managerial class to mobilize itself.

Summary

Any corporation deciding to launch a turn up initiative must not do so willy-nilly. A general roadmap of six sequential steps ought to be followed.

CHAPTER 5
CHANGING GOVERNANCE

Responsible Governance
Not Warped Boards

One meaning of "warp" is to guide a ship, and boards that let their owners' corporate ships run afoul are not all uncommon. [1] A warped board, in short, holds the wrong view of what corporate performance should mean; lets the wrong CEO be chosen; lets the corporation be misled and mismanaged; and allows lavish rewards for negative successes and even negative failures. With this kind of board in place short performance, or negative manner of doing business and negative failures and negative successes, gets a head start and never looks back.

Straightening out warped boards requires getting the right directors and adopting the right board process. There can't be one without the other if a public corporation is to look and to act like a corporation dedicated to tall performance.

Getting the Right Directors

When new board members are to be selected, several issues need to be resolved regarding membership criteria; outsiders versus insiders, CEO outsiders, CEO/chair duality, relevant personalities, multiple board memberships, term limits, and level of financial expertise desired.

Selecting Mostly Outsider Board Members

The argument for outsiders is that their independence of CEOs will enable them to actually guide and even, if necessary, veto CEO decisions instead of rubberstamping them. At the same time, in making boards more independent care needs to be taken to avoid creating adversarial and legalistic confrontations with their CEOs. Neither lapdogs nor bulldogs will ever help steer corporations toward tall performance.

The Sarbanes-Oxley Act, established in response to Enron's collapse and the other major corporate scandals of that period, requires boards to have a majority of outside members. However, as I believe Congress knew, not only was the majority of Enron's board outsiders, but the board had suspended its conflict-of-interest guidelines! [2] So outsiders are in name only when CEOs do what they did before the law, ensure that outsiders are picked who are more dependent than independent. Enron's board members had contractual and other kinds of potentially compromising ties to the corporation. [3]

The argument for outside directors, nevertheless, remains logically sound and should be heeded. All board members but two should be truly independent outsiders. One of the outsiders should represent a long-term institutional investor to help resist myopic decisions. The insider besides the CEO should be a veteran non-executive member who is widely recognized for his or her superlative performance and has a legitimate and long-term stake in the corporation's future. To Marjorie Kelly, former editor of Business Ethics, "worker governance is a fundamental pillar of democratizing our economy—a truth we hold to be self-evident." [4] Her views are entirely consistent with my rationale for lowerarchies of responsibly empowered people.

The Sarbanes-Oxley Act does not require employee representation on boards because corporate lobbyists managed to get a provision for it stricken from a draft of the legislation. Shareholder resolutions for worker governance have been futile. In a proxy statement I once received was a resolution calling for union representation that was easily defeated when confronted with management's argument that "the interests of shareholders would not be served by electing representatives of special interest groups." What a self-serving rationalization! Shareholders are a "special interest group." A bigger one, of course, is any management that wants lapdog boards and gets them by basically dictating board memberships. What with the clamor for board reform and increasing shareholder lawsuits, however, I think we may be witnessing the slow end of subservience.

Barring CEO Outsiders

Is it really a good idea for some outsiders to be current CEOs of other corporations? The argument for picking a few is that colloquially speaking they have been there and done that. But there are at least two arguments more compelling against doing so. By virtue of their stature and experience they would probably yield too much influence during board deliberations, which might be felt the most in the hubris of good times and the anxiety of bad times. And, as the chair of a think tank and advocacy organization once said, "Too many boards are composed of current and former CEOs who have a vested interest in maintaining a system that is beneficial to them."[5] To me, this second argument is a clincher. The board should not have a vested interest in the corpocracy!

Barring CEO from being Board Chair

Notwithstanding the advisability of making the CEO and board relationship one of a collaborative partnership,

47

despite evidence that who chairs the board is of no consequence, and despite the ludicrous argument that splitting the CEO/chair duality "risks sending mixed signals to the market regarding who really is in charge at the top," it makes absolutely no sense to me for the top manager to sit atop the owners' board even if the top manager owns a lot of the company's stock. [6] At best it is a non sequitur. At worst, it puts in an influential seat an influential insider who probably has the greatest conflict of interest.

Seeking Agreeably Disagreeable Board Personalities

Too much agreeability is not good for any board working together as a team. Instead, being "agreeably disagreeable" whenever there are substantive differences of opinion and playing devil's advocate to prevent unanimity from being stupidity ought to be encouraged. "The highest performing companies," says Jeffrey Sonnefeld, drawing on his governance research spanning more than a quarter of a century, "have extremely contentious boards that regard dissent as an obligation and treat no subject as undiscussable." [7]

Minimizing Multiple Board Memberships

When Enron imploded most of its outside directors were on other boards as well, a common occurrence when memberships are handed out like honoraria with no strings attached other than to go along for the ride and not rock the boat. [8] Directors should not serve on more than one board. Governing a corporation seeking tall performance is far too important a responsibility to allow directors to spread themselves too thinly.

Avoiding Term Limits

Term limits are an eligibility issue because boards need to decide how long members should be allowed to serve, barring termination for cause. Term limits, it has been argued, "keep the board fresh." [9] Well, boards are not like fish. Too short a term limit may be more of a problem because of disruption in the continuity of teamwork within the board and between it and the CEO. Term limits seem no different from a mandatory retirement age. Both criteria are arbitrary rather than being dependent on performance considerations of each case. Flexibility in handling the matter would seem to be a better option because of changing circumstances and variability among individual cases. A transition to a new CEO, for instance, might be an opportune time to discuss whether any board changes would also be desirable.

Avoiding Picking Financial Wizards

Although the SEC requires financial expertise on the board's audit committee, even there a working level of knowledge will usually suffice, a big drop below expertise, should be sufficient. Advises one former dean of a business graduate school, if "there's a transaction underway that's so complicated [the board] can't understand it,---that's the point at which you need to get an expert to come in and look at what it's all about and what the effects are." [10] Precisely! Know enough as a board member to know when something looks fishy or too good to be true and then to consult with someone who is an expert.

Even if expertise were essential it can be compromised. Take the case of Enron's board pilloried right and left since the corporation's implosion. [11] The board oozed with expertise, [12] "No [other] corporation," said one authority on governance matters, "could have had more appropriate financial competencies and experience on its board." [13] The expertise, however, apparently had been compromised. A business reporter, after reviewing the "mind-numbing details" and "damning conclusions" of a six-month probe by a Senate panel, observed that "Again and again, the red flags went up. Again and again, they were ignored." [14]

Summary

Warped boards of directors, the handpicked cronies of imperialistic CEOs, would sleep their way through the grounding of the corporate ship if government didn't keep it afloat. Numerous recommendations are made for straightening up those boards.

CHAPTER 6
CHANGING LEADERSHIP

The Right CEO for a Corporate Turn Up

Irresponsible CEO's and boards Business Week contended in a feature article a few years ago "are arguably the most serious challenge facing Corporate America today." [1] It is indeed arguable. To me, the biggest challenge will be corporate survival should the corpocracy ever be ended. But, yes, Business Week is right as long as the corpocracy continues to exist.

Personal flaws may be the single most important source of CEO failure. These flaws, five in particular I have concluded from my extensive review of the literature, can be destructive when the person who has them is in a position of power and within the corpocracy. It is a fast-acting stimulant for personal vulnerabilities to surge to the forefront. "If you're not careful, you'll be seduced," is the way a former CEO of Westinghouse Electric Corporation put it in an interview with Business Week. [2] The five are greed, irresponsibility and lack of virtue, materialistic values, moral frailty, narcissism (including unbridled hubris), and narrow-mindedness. They usually go together. A person with one tends to have all of the rest, too. The five are not unique to the corner office but are more pronounced and more destructive there.

How does a corporation start over with the right CEO? The firing of CEOs, albeit almost always with extravagant going-away gifts, is not uncommon. CEO failure is also a board failure. It hired or let be hired the wrong CEO. But boards rarely have a substantial say in the CEO's successor.

51

Moreover, the successor typically is as bad as the predecessor. If that were not the case, and we see instances of it almost daily, there would be no corpocracy. The right CEOs would tell government, "thanks but no thanks. We don't need your hand outs, we don't want any part of war mongering or profiteering, and we don't need 'stay out of jail cards' because tall performance is our standard."

Given an ejected CEO, a board should avoid being burned again by searching and choosing a new CEO very carefully. The board's nominating committee ought to have a pretty good idea of what kind of a CEO to avoid, but not necessarily the kind to seek.

There may be no subjects studied, written, and talked about more than leadership (in graduate school eons ago I studied under a professor who spearheaded a tern year study of leadership). Literally thousands of research studies have tried to fathom the subject. So too have poets, playwrights, historians, and pundits of all stripes. Today there are at least a dozen different theories of leadership that have been espoused by serious scholars. I just recently reviewed for publication a new one and my critique wasn't very favorable. [3]

Five Prized Attributes for CEOs

From my literature reviews over the years I have identified five "prized" attributes that any CEO or any other leader should possess. They are integrity, wisdom, humility, shared leadership, and a liberal arts education.

1. Integrity. It has been convincingly said that leadership has a tremendous impact on an organization's "ethics center of gravity."[4] No further elaboration from me is needed here.

2. Wisdom

My concept of wisdom is close to what Dr. John Churchill, secretary of Phi Bata Kappa, considers are the attributes essential to citizenship: critical thought in order to understand and evaluate deliberations, knowledge of the relevant facts to guide the deliberations, and knowing what is worth deliberating. [5] His lofty criteria, which look like they come right out of the Golden Age of Greece, not only set the bar high for citizenship but also for board members and CEOs!

One who leaped high over the bar was the late J. Irwin Miller who never went to business school and at the age of twenty five began building a failing diesel company into a Fortune 500 company. He was eulogized as "the industrial-strength humanist who knew how to get things built." Grounded in the liberal arts at Yale his maturing "wisdom and values" and his ability to apply them to new fields made him, the eulogizer continued, the modern-day equivalent of a Thomas Jefferson.[6] The most effective leaders," one business professor steeped in the subject has found, "see themselves as builders and humanists."[7] I wonder if Miller was one of their role models.

3. Humility

A CEO wrote the following letter to the chair of his company's compensation committee asking to be paid less:

> *---the company had a terrific year---however, I do not feel my own performance was as strong as in previous years---therefore I would like to see the bulk of my direct reports, and many of their direct reports, paid greater bonuses than I receive.*

Ethan Berman had not intended for his letter to be publicized, but a former SEC chair very critical of excessive CEO pay got a copy and, finding it so extraordinary, sent it on to a New York Times columnist. [8] And I also found it so extraordinary that I had to mention it here. A narcissist would never write such a letter in a blue moon.

Humility puts the brakes on any surging egotism. Humility is the opposite of hubris that goes hand in hand with the egotism of leaders heady with power.

4. Shared Leadership

Nothing could be more fitting for the corporate model I am proposing in this book than a leader "at the top" who has whatever attributes it takes, including substantive experiences to share the leadership. Leadership is "romanticized" in corporate America. [9] Boards have tended to seek charismatic CEOs, usually white knights, who can come charging in to take charge and hopefully save the tall, besieged castle.

Shared leadership, on the other hand, is the exact opposite. It is a group phenomenon in particular contexts rather than an individual phenomenon of a single, would-be "savior." There are three characteristics of shared leadership. It is distributed and interdependent. It is embodied in social interaction. And thirdly, its outcomes include "mutual learning, greater shared understanding, and eventually, positive action." [10]

5. Liberal Arts Education

Wisdom, integrity, humility, and shared leadership generally are the kind of attributes of people who get a liberal arts education instead of or before getting any business schools education. The humanities courses in a liberal arts curriculum are simply incompatible with the values and assumptions about human nature underlying a business education. [11]

Over 35 years ago a controversial article appeared in the Harvard Business Review that would soon become one of the journal's hottest pieces. [12] The authors, two Harvard Business School professors, contended that the American manager had become a portfolio manager, with narrowed training and experience, often in finance or law, having no product allegiance, savvy, or imagination, and very myopic in vision. Their gloomy assessment apparently remains valid today. Even the body that accredits business schools is critical of their narrow curriculum and heavy reliance on case studies and textbooks. [13]

One effect of loading the curriculum with quantitative, finance oriented subjects, including emphasis on the conventional bottom line, to the near exclusion of the qualitative subjects, is to further handicap students who bring their materialistic value orientations with them to business school. When they graduate, they are ill-prepared to consider the long-term, social, and ethical considerations in making business decisions. A study by the Aspen Institute of approximately 2,000 graduates of the top business schools concluded that getting an education from them not only didn't improve the morality of the students, but weakened it. [14] It's noteworthy that the scandalous Enron was overflowing with MBA graduates. [15]

Searching for the Right CEO

Within large corporations there is typically in place a replacement and succession planning process for filling key managerial and executive slots once they are vacated. It may start with junior-level assessment centers to select people for management development programs and continue on to leadership development programs. Somewhere along the way this elongated process may turn into a succession of tournaments favoring backstabbing Machiavellians. [16] When that happens, the ultimate winner so shaped by the process very likely will be a misshaped CEO.

The tournament syndrome aside, this process is totally unsuitable for any lowerarchy that has no managerial classes and few successive layers. But this process isn't even advisable for hierarchies in my opinion. It is costly, consuming billions of dollars yearly and very wasteful if it is true that managerial incompetence is so prevalent. [17] The process is also misconceived and misdirected. By conceiving leadership as an individual phenomenon individuals are developed rather than conceiving leadership as a group phenomenon and developing leadership more broadly.

Leadership development, it has been argued, should be aimed at creating through experiential learning and reflective practice a "leaderful" organization that would be a "gateway to collective leadership." [18] The argument goes hand in glove with the shared leadership theory. Obviously, making the argument is easier than making what is argued happen. It should happen because billions of dollars are wasted yearly on leadership development that leads to what, further entrenching the corporation as a member of the corpocracy?
So where does the foregoing leave the corporation in finding a CEO inside the corporation? Is a "collective" or

leadership-sharing CEO out of the question, and if not, how do candidates get primed for it? It is only out of the question if a lowerarchy of responsibly empowered teams is out of the question. As for the second part of the question, consider this very sketchy scenario. Teams share and/or rotate leadership roles. Teams nominate or pick core process leaders. Together they pick or nominate business unit leaders. And so this process continues until a few individuals are selected to serve as rotating apprentice CEOs who learn through practice how to be a CEO. Conceivably they might all become qualified to be the real CEO.

Hiring an outside CEO whether the person is a rent-a-CEO like a turnaround artist or any ordinary CEO is a bad option. They cannot possibly develop a sense of loyalty and stewardship for their limited time at the helm and will not make long-term investments for the sake of the corporation's future well-being.

Recruiting CEOs from outside, moreover, is a pathetic reflection on either the quality of internal capabilities or the board and CEO's inattention to them. But if a search for CEO candidates outside the corporation is made, the searchers need to focus on the same prized attributes and try to acquire and scrutinize the track records of the candidates. The records of outside candidates obviously will not be as readily available or probably as complete and reliable as those of inside candidates.

Summary

Sitting in the corner offices of most corporations are the wrong kinds of CEOs. You should not want them to lead you or any organization in which you have a stake. This chapter tells what to do about it.

CHAPTER 7
CHANGING BOARD AND LEADERSHIP CUSTOMS

Changing faces at the top won't matter much if corporate customs don't change. There's a lot of momentous decision making still ahead for the people at the top assuming they have gotten this far, and these decisions will require some wrenching changes in perspectives and practice. A new CEO once said he "had to let go of every dearly held management concept he had developed over the decades as a manager." [1] And he was only spearheading a turnaround! I'm certain he should not have adopted whatever new management concepts he did adopt. The turn up initiative requires people in business to think very differently about what management means. You will see what I mean as we go along in this book.

Board Meetings:
Adopting Different Protocol

The board needs to hold a series of board meetings to do some very unconventional reviewing and rethinking about the corporation. It would be unconventional because the task at hand is corporate turn up, not turn around. The meetings are hardly an academic exercise. The corporation's future is at stake.

Because the board would be breaking new ground the meetings need to be guided by a new protocol. A director, not the CEO should lead the meetings. There would be an expert facilitator. Domination or intimidation by anyone would not be allowed. Open mindedness, candor, and respect for differences of opinion would be encouraged. To discourage groupthink, members would rotate in a devil's advocate role.

The board would encourage input from the largest shareholder, a workforce representative, the largest supplier, the largest customer, and an official from the community where the corporation has its biggest operations. Suddenly being more transparent and inclusive in this clearly signals that the board is seriously considering steering the corporation on a new path.

Adopting Real Meaning of Success and Failure

Adopting the real meaning of success and failure is a prerequisite for launching a turn up initiative. The corporation must be liberated from the conventional bottom line mentality and custom. It provides mainly the pressure and the government provides mainly the temptations to do business in an infinite variety of wrongdoings, legal and illegal ones.

Reviewing and Reorienting
Corporate Purpose, Vision, and Values

Corporate purpose is the corporation's reason to exist. Corporate purpose also helps to give the corporation its identity-"this is who we are and what we do;" it influences performance and its management (different purposes have different effects on performance), and is the root of the corporation's vision. In rethinking the corporation's purpose the board needs to decide whether it should only be to make money and maximize shareholder wealth in following a course of unsustainable growth? Or should it be to benefit other stakeholders as well and to cause no harm to anyone or anything in following a course of sustainable development? Only a purpose like the second one is consistent with a turn up toward tall performance.

A vision courts change by asking questions like, "What would we like to see ourselves become and do in, say, five to ten years from now?" To be consistent with the company's purpose part of the board's answer must be, "we want to be by then a truly great company!" Simply being the best in the corporation's industry is simply not great enough of a vision. Clearly, vision must not outstrip reason or reality. Much has been written about the failures of visions and visionaries. [2] But there is no reason why tall performance cannot serve as an inspiring vision.

Corporate values reflect what is really important to people in the corporation, especially people in the upper reaches of the corporate hierarchy. Corporate values are an important feature of the corporation's culture (see Chapter 9) and help predispose the behavior of people in the corporation. There are two fundamental kinds of values, instrumental values and end values. Instrumental values speak to one part of tall performance, the manner (i.e. behavior) in which ends are pursued. End values speak to the other part, positive results consistent with corporate purpose. There must be a consensus in the meetings that both positive success and positive failure will be valued, negative success and negative failure will not be valued, and all of the universal ethical values will be honored in practice throughout the corporation.

Reviewing Corporate Performance Equation

Corporate	+	Situational	=	Corporate	+	Corporate
Inputs		Inputs		Behavior		Results

This part of the agenda would be quite unlike a review of financial facts and figures about the corporation's performance. We would expect even warped boards and flawed CEOs to have some sense of at least some of the facts and figures, albeit deliberately distorted as they sometimes are. But the agenda proposed here would start with the input side of the corporation's performance equation, not its output side.

Something like an "input scoreboard" needs to be made that shows for each pair of inputs listed in Chapter 3 which one is the corporation's input. An understanding is reached of why the tall inputs are essential. Operational inputs such as technological development and marketing strategies are brought up at another time. They are important, of course, but their effectiveness is to no small measure dependent on the inputs listed. As we shall see, for example, a hierarchy is no place where innovation can flourish.

The agenda should turn next to an examination of every aspect of the output side. Besides the usual review of the corporation's financial performance, an intense and candid probe of corporate behavior is needed that looks for answers to such questions as: "When have we sacrificed corporate integrity for profit?" "To what extent have we relied on government handouts and hands-off policies?" "How often have we appeared in press and for what? What harm has our corporation caused one or more groups of stakeholders, including the environment either directly or indirectly? Have there been any consumer boycotts or other kinds of protests about the way we do business? Just how far from tall performance is our performance?"

Rethinking and Reorienting
Corporate Leadership, Power, and Control

A typically imperialistic CEO doesn't share his or her leadership responsibilities, hoards power (much of it provided by government), and exercises obsessively tight control. Such behavior might be tolerable if the CEO's performance contributed substantially to the corporation's positive success, but that is seldom the case. Corporations tend to fare for better or worse not so much on the performance of their CEOs but on the performance of most of the other people in them, on economic and market sector conditions, and on sheer corporate size. [3] A different perspective and practice are thus needed on the inseparable components of the corporation's leadership, power, and control.

The traditional paradigm equates leadership with control and the organizational structure that enables control, namely, the hierarchy. Because the turn up initiative requires turning the hierarchy into a lowerarchy, the vertical chain of command and control gives way to responsible empowerment of the workforce, a dramatic departure from the customary way of organizing for and doing business. No one person can effectively be omnipresent and omnipotent in today's complex and racing world. Unfortunately, a CEO honest enough to acknowledge this and humble enough to stop hoarding and exercising control, or power, is not the common variety CEO.

Rethinking and Reorienting
Corporate Stance Toward Society in General

Surrounded by and part of America's corpocracy the corporation's CEO and board need to make the extraordinary decision to write the corporation's own social charter with self-imposed restrictions (e.g., no externalizing of costs such as from pollution, no outsourcing of jobs, etc.) aimed at serving society, not exploiting it. Two other extraordinary decisions would also need to be made, one to close down the corporate social responsibility program and the other to discontinue corporate philanthropy. At first blush these two decisions seem anti-social, so I will take a moment to explain why they are anything but anti-social.

Closing Down the Social Responsibility Program

Some time ago Novo Nordisk, the Danish global pharmaceutical company, adopted "triple bottom line" accounting to its business activities. [4] The approach has since become a familiar term that is also commonly known as corporate social responsibility or CSR for short. It refers to a firm's accountability for its financial, social, and environmental performance. Public backlash and activism by NGO's to corporate wrongdoing in no small measure furthered the CSR movement.

CSR is mostly a façade. Corporations set up and trumpet their CSR programs to divert the public's eye from corporate misdeeds and corporate welfare. Corporations give CSR little more than lip service, seeing it as nothing more than an inexpensive propagandizing opportunity to divert attention from their still doing business as usual. [5] CSR, moreover, is a superfluous concept in light of what should be the corporate bottom line of ethics below which a corporation should refrain from going. A firm cannot spoil

63

the environment ethically any more than it can harm society ethically. A firm that is ethically responsible is socially responsible, ipso facto.

CSR can also be counterproductive if the corporation gets distracted from what it should be doing in responding to CSR advocates; if the corporation undertakes sham or misleading CSR initiatives to mask wrongdoing; or if CSR advocates go too far and pressure the corporation to undertake initiatives that risk causing shareholder lawsuits for fiduciary irresponsibility. Corporations simply need to act ethically, but their ethics programs (see Chapter 9) are as much window dressing as are their philanthropy and CSR programs.

Discontinuing Corporate Philanthropy

Does corporate philanthropy make up for opportunities lost for the general welfare because of corporate welfare? Corporate welfare apologists would have us think so. Don't be fooled. This argument needs to be unmasked for what it is, a diversion, a dissimilitude, and a devious exploitation.

The roots of corporate philanthropy in America, I think, can be traced to the "guilt gifts" from the robber barons of the Gilded Age. Corporations today continue to give billions of dollars annually to charities often with self-serving motives as when, for instance, the gifts are aimed at benefiting board members. [6] Some charities are fakes set up to funnel donations to political patrons. Journalist Eric Lipton reports that "charities set up by a score of lawmakers from both parties have become an important — and completely unregulated — way for corporations and lobbyists to get their voices heard and to curry favor on Capitol Hill."[7]

Aside from some outstanding museums and performing arts centers that owe their existence to corporate philanthropists, most do more harm than good. This was the opinion of Andrew Carnegie, one of the original philanthropists, and it was recently reinforced in interviews with grantees. [8] The interviewer found a "huge gap" between giver intentions and the effects of the process and the grants. Grantees were typically treated disrespectfully, were hamstrung by red tape, and questioned both the "priorities and strategies "of the grantors.

Rethinking and Reorienting
Corporate Stance Toward the Marketplace

Two very different types of marketplace coexist. In the first transactions involve real goods and services. In the second transactions involve using money to make more money. An ancient thinker on economics, Aristotle, was very disdainful of the second type. So am I and so should anyone who favors a productive society in which everyone enjoys the fruits of their labor and has a sufficient standard of living. This kind of society cannot and does not exist in America that is being driven, downwards, partly by speculative capitalism.

It is a travesty to treat speculative capitalists fixated on corporate quarterly earnings as the "owners" of corporations in which they invest. They are no more like owners than the renters at the sea-side summer condominium where my wife and I owned a unit. We never rented. We could see the damage done by renters of the owners' units versus the care taken by the non-renting owners of their own units. Speculators care only about tomorrow's stock price and not at all about the corporation's longevity and well-being of its other stakeholders.

In responding to both the temptations and pressures of Wall Street's conventional bottom line, corporate executives resort to all sorts of wrongdoing. Veteran reporter of banking and finance news and former editor of US Banker, Robert A. Bennett, concluded after more than forty years of accumulating anecdotal evidence that the pressure of consistently showing increases in quarterly earnings leads to cutting ethical corners in order to "hit the numbers" promised and expected.[9]

Toward the Investment Community

There are several options for dealing with owners and the investment community at large. The corporation could stop being speculative and greedy itself in using equity as part of its compensation. Some targeted stock marketing could be aimed away from speculators. [10] The forecasting of quarterly earnings to Wall Street could be discontinued and the rationale for the corporation's new direction explained. [11] The corporation could choose to support challenges of state statues that put shareholders' rights first (as has been done in more than half of the states) while also choosing to simply interpret the statutes more broadly and creatively. It could choose to support proposals to reform the very nature of capitalism, changing it from undemocratic to democratic capitalism. [12] And, finally, it could decide to go private if there is a friendly and munificent buyer who will take the corporation off the market. A CEO once wistfully exclaimed that if she could take it private to avoid those pressures she would have done it yesterday. [13] Another CEO did exactly that when his corporation found a friendly buyer, allowing the CEO "[not to] worry about this month, this quarter or this year and usually [to] put 90 percent of our earnings back into the company every year-that's something that would be very difficult to do for a public company." [14]

Toward the Global Market

A salient element of the marketplace of either type is its globalization. It means different things to different people and has different effects on different people. In its simplest sense, globalization means the presence of and imprint on other countries by another country's agents. Globalization is controversial because of its imprints. Some claim their net effect is positive, some say negative. My conclusion is that the net effect is unquestionably negative due to the widening gap between the haves and the have-nots, the exploitation of nearly free labor and natural resources like minerals and oil, the high jacking of countries' sovereignties, the outsourcing of jobs via international trade agreements, and the increasing degradation of global ecology.

But the net effect does not have to be a negative one and, in any case, globalization however it is practiced in whatever of its three forms (political, social, and commercial) is here to stay. The corporation needs to rethink the issues involved and what would be the proper role of the corporation. If the corporation is a multinational corporation with a global presence it has already had a heavy and mostly negative imprint. The board and CEO need to do an about face on this issue.

Toward Other Corporations

Any large corporation does business with other corporations within the same industry and in other industries. Any corporation pursuing tall performance is obligated to create and/or take opportunities to be a role model in how it deals not only in any transactions but also in public relations with corporate America at large and particular industries and corporations. While taking the lead in opposing the corpocracy in one or more ways the corporation's secondary concern has to be trying to create a "level playing field" within the corporation's own industry so that, for instance, the most competitive corporations do not gain an unbeatable advantage by, say, continuing to be a welfare queen and amassing profit without honor.

Toward Government

This may be the toughest item on the agenda bar none. Like mother and infant, government and big business need each other in a corpocracy. If corporate lifelines to its captive government were to be cut, the corpocracy would atrophy and dependent corporations would flounder.

The reality that those lifelines "maintain" an even playing field among competitors is a formidable barrier to any widespread reforms. How many boards and CEOs will rethink the respective roles of business and government in a democracy as envisioned by its founders? How many CEOs will then step forward and declare that from now on their corporations will not only stop exploiting the government but will also support the legal, political, and social reforms to end the corpocracy? How lonely must be Howard Shultz, the CEO of Startbucks who appears to be no ordinary CEO. He recently called "on his fellow CEOs -- and other would-be donors -- to boycott all campaign contributions to either party until the nation's elected leaders put aside their political posturing and find some common ground on long-term fiscal issues." [15] While he could have gone further and called for a total end to the corpocracy, he's on the right track, and any corporation must stay on it if tall performance is the goal.

Reviewing and Reorienting
Corporate Decision Making

People in the lower reaches of a hierarchy rarely make non-routine decisions and rarely know what is being decided by people at the top. Jeffrey Nielson, author of The Myth of Leadership, tells the story of his encounter with-count them-the big chiefs of a certain corporation; the CEO, the CFO, the COO, the CIO, and the chief of staff! He had only 10 minutes on the agenda to tell the chiefs that his internal survey showed that throughout every level of the corporation people were frustrated over "not being given the opportunity to participate in decision making." And what was the response from that crowded room of overlords? "People will whine, always have, always will." To them, the survey's feedback was simply evidence of "the inevitable complaints of unmotivated workers stung by "tough" leadership decisions." [16]

What exactly are "tough" decisions? I would say there are two kinds and they aren't mutually exclusive. One is tough ethical decision making as in deciding for example whether to forego or penalize negative success. The other are the really momentous, "big bet" kind of decisions such as deciding whether to enter a new market, whether to buy another corporation, and the like. A professor of management sciences who has written a book on the subject concluded that "half of the decisions fail," and "almost always" because of blunders by the decision makers and not because of bad luck or situational factors." [17] But I would qualify the professor's conclusion. There is at least one situational factor guaranteed to yield flawed and sometimes disastrous decisions. This factor is the hierarchy. It is an internal situation that predisposes "tough" leadership decisions to undesirable outcomes.

The corporation's record of momentous decisions made needs to be reviewed, who made them, the process followed in making them, and their outcomes. Particular attention needs to be paid to the narrowness of the perspectives leading up to the decisions. Bad decisions, especially those that require cutting ethical corners in carrying out the decisions invariably are made with too narrow of a perspective, that is, too shortsighted and too exclusive. Decisions made solely by the people in the upper reaches of a hierarchy are bound to have a narrow perspective if for no other reason than that these people are too far removed from realities such as not getting foreboding news from the lower reaches.

Decision making can never be the same again on a corporate climb to tall performance. How can it be when the top is no longer the top or the sole maker of momentous decisions and when all decision makers when making decisions must bear in mind the standard of tall performance? The board and the CEO need to tackle head on the issue of what types of decisions if any will be the sole prerogative of the board and/or the CEO and other senior executives. Should, as was the case for a while in one corporation, "non-leaders" make some 99% of important decisions? [18] In a hierarchy, needless to say, the answer is a thunderous No! Decision making there stays top down! Momentous decisions are unilaterally made at the top. Lesser decisions are made at the middle. Few if any decisions are left for the bottom. This is befitting for the quite arrogant, self-serving, and not uncommon view that "management is decision making." [19] But it would be very ill-fitting for a corporation on the way to becoming a lowerarchy.

No less crucial an issue than where decisions are to be made is the process of making decisions regardless of where they are made. The process should essentially be uniform corporate-wide. Three requirements need to be satisfied in shaping, but not cementing the process: take a double-time perspective; avoid group think; and limited time search.

Taking a Double-Tme Perspective

Taking a "double-time" perspective in making big decisions involves considering the time taken to make the decision, and the time line of possible consequences. Too much time becomes the familiar paralysis by analysis problem. Too little time causes the common rush-to-judgment blunder. [20] What the long-term consequences of the decision might be should always be considered. Lawrence Mitchell, author of Corporate Irresponsibility reels off a litany of the adverse effects of shortsighted decisions and myopic managing: a volatile stock market turned into a casino, under investment in training and R & D, layoffs, plant closings, alienated workers, unsafe products, and a polluted environment. [21]

Avoiding Group Think

The second requirement is to avoid group think. History is strewn with the disasters of unquestioning deference to the predominant view. The best way to keep this from happening is to program into the process a role for a devil's advocate, an insistence on a lively debate, and also an insistence that the next and related requirement be met.

Avoiding the Limited Search Trap

The last requirement is to avoid the "limited search trap" in which for one reason or another, but none of the reasons being a right one, minds are closed to other options. [22]

71

By their very nature momentous decisions are not single-option issues. A turn up initiative will require a corporation in its future decision making to broaden the search for all reasonable as well as what may seem to be unreasonable options, to become well informed about them, and to set aside self-serving interests in picking an option.

Summary

This chapter began by noting that changing faces at the top won't matter much if corporate customs don't change. Customary behavior is basically habitual behavior, doing the same things as a matter of routine. A turn up initiative requires very different behavior to become the custom, including how the corporation will make important decisions and its perspectives and stance toward important situational inputs such as the investment community, government, and the like.

CHAPTER 8
BECOMING A LOWERARCHY

The hierarchy, or pyramid, has been around as the predominant "architectural" model for large organizations in government, religion, and business at least since Ch'in, the "First Exhalted Emperor, established a hierarchical bureaucracy to control the newly unified China at least two millennia ago. The hierarchy's ubiquity and longevity can hardly be attributed to some natural law of organization. Biologists tell us that hierarchies are not natural phenomena. [1] The corporate hierarchy is strictly a human invention. Nor can the ubiquity and longevity of hierarchies be attributed to their performance. Tall performance is impossible in a tall organization. It has too many shortcomings.

Why Not a Hierarchy?

The Hierarchy's False Premises

Hierarchies are built on six false premises that became hard core beliefs over time. The first is the so-called "Theory X" view that workers are lazy, dishonest, incapable, intractable, and untrustworthy and thus need to be assigned the simplest work and be closely supervised. The second, known as the span of control premise, presumes there is a limit to how many people one person can control at the next lower layer, thought to be seven or eight. The third is that business operations require both simplification and specialization of work. Routine work is atomized into repetitive tasks. Non routine work is sorted out and put into specialties. The fourth is that work should be organized into fixed positions with specific duties and tasks. The fifth is that management is first and foremost a managerial class of people rather than a process for managing performance. The last premise is that bigger is better.

These premises made sense to the new industrialists and their advisors during the industrial revolution and so corporations grew tall and big, a trend that was accelerated early in America by relaxing the requirements for the chartering of public corporations. But these premises should never have made sense. Moreover, despite arguable progress in the making of goods and services over the years, these premises in several ways make achieving tall performance impossible.

Hierarchies Have Many Layers Adding No Value

The hierarchy's many layers are "throughputs," not outputs that really matter to the "front line" where product or service meets the customer. People perched on any layer and who cause problems look to other layers for placing blame. Layering creates a chain of command and control, and the commanded and controlled people lose their initiative. Layering requires costly caring and feeding of the managerial class and constipates the business process. Communication gets distorted with just too many mouths and ears on top of each other, made worse when each of their heads has its own separate agenda. Layering thwarts quality improvements in services and products. People are concentrating more on managing their careers up the ladder and lose sight of managing the corporation's performance.

Hierarchies Are Overly Compartmentalized

The false premises lead to excessive compartmentalization such as thousands of occupied positions. They are tiny compartments that effectively imprison potential by narrowly prescribing roles and responsibilities; provide the excuse, "it's not my job;" require a complicated and costly position classification system; and, because management is considered first and foremost a position rather than a process, provide jobs for far too many managers.

Other compartments are the classical corporate silos or functional departments (e.g., procurement, inventory, engineering, manufacturing, etc.), each with its own layering, its own goals, its rivalries and blame games with the other departments, its impossible coordination with the other departments, and its substandard contribution to overall performance.

Hierarchies are Too Big

Corporations tend to grow too big partly because of the false premise that bigger is better, which in turn is based on several rationales such as the belief that economy of scale lowers costs and raises efficiency and the belief that product and market diversification is more profitable or at least more enduring than is market specialization. Additionally, corporations grow too big because of layering and compartmentalization.

Bigness hampers performance. Bigness, for instance, keeps the corporation from being more agile and innovative. Bigness, however, is good, not bad for corporate members of the corpocracy. Why is that? Two reasons; they thrive on government handouts and thus do not need to perform better; and they can operate illegally with little worry about accountability because of the government's hands-off policies. Indeed, if this corporate welfare and immunity were to cease, so too would today's corporations unless they reformed themselves.

Hierarchies Can't Empower the Workforce

The workforce is the lowest layer on the pecking order; actually with no pecking rights at all. There are so many commands and controls coming from the top and its subordinate layers of management. Responsibly empowered workers in the rare and short-lived cases where they can be found (e.g., in experiments with self-managed teams in a small part of a large corporation) will invariably outperform commanded and controlled people. Responsible empowerment requires self-control and implies a span of responsibility, not a span of control for each person.

Hierarchies are Structurally Tall, Morally Short

The hierarchy's very foundation is the unethical premise that the doers, or "jackasses," at the bottom can be exploited and are dispensable because they are neither smart enough nor enterprising enough to be of any greater value. [2] Instead of fulfilling both a moral and an economic obligation to create a short organizational structure full of empowered people, empire-building management erects a vertical chain of command and control that enlivens the unethical premise and enslaves the workforce all the while hypocritically professing the critical importance of the organization's "human capital" and giving lip service to empowerment. [3]

The hierarchy is an ideal place for cowardly sycophants and liars who send false information up the chain to curry favor or to protect their rear ends. While that feature is more of an economic and less of a moral drawback, the reverse flow of messages in the form of ignoble expectations is worse from a moral standpoint. These expectations cascade downwards until fulfilled, and the

76

vertical distance separating the original source of the expectations from the actual wrongdoing plus the fragmented responsibility along the way makes it easier for the original source to feign ignorance and dodge accountability. It sometimes takes dogged determination, like that of the judge in the following true vignette, to get at the real culprits perched high up in the chain:

> The company was caught dumping over
> 75,000 gallons of carcinogenic chemicals
> into Puget Sound. The judge refused to
> hear the guilty plea of lawyers sent by
> the company. "Bring the company's leader,"
> he ordered, "the public is entitled to know
> who is responsible." Three executives were
> sent. "No," he said, "I want the top officer
> here." Finally, the chairman and the CEO
> appeared in court. [4]

Until caught, the real culprits in this case thought they had managed not to get their hands dirty. To cut costs, they had issued an ignoble expectation that eventually landed in the hands of the dumpers, who were being nicely rewarded with upside down incentives. And it didn't matter to the judge whether the CEO knew about the expectations or whether they originated a bit lower. The judge probably presumed that the CEO was sending all kinds of edicts and signals about cutting costs and no edicts about what boundaries to stay within, and besides, the buck stops at the top in any case.

Becoming a Lowerarchy

Just how flat or short does a hierarchy need to get before it becomes a lowerarchy? There is nothing shorter than flat I would imagine. But being flat is not essential for a corporate lowerarchy.

No two lowerarchies will be exactly alike in their organizational structure yet each must follow the prescription below if tall performance is to have a chance. They are bare-bone because there needs to be wide latitude in designing the lowerarchy and modifying it in a constantly changing environment.

Keeping Only Valued Layers

Eliminating value-subtracting layers raises two obvious questions when setting out to lower a hierarchy. One is "how do we determine what is or would be a value-subtracting layer?" Any layer that does a lot of commanding and controlling and makes little or no substantive contribution to tall performance ought to be eliminated.

The other question is "what do we do with the people perched on layers to be eliminated? Several years ago the highest priority of the incoming CEO of one large corporation was to down size the company. [5] Some 35,000 managerial and non-managerial people were axed. That is a lot of heads rolling. Poetic justice would call for turning the span of control upside down: for every employee felled, fell at least seven managers!

Downsizing is rarely effective. It is not a carefully conceived plan at all but instead a knee-jerk reaction to not having a plan. Boeing, for instance, reportedly has a history of "back-and-forth firings and hiring's of workers" apparently with no lessons learned in between. [6]

78

There are many ways to cut costs without cutting people, and it is important to remember that lowering a hierarchy requires eliminating echelons of managerial positions, not people. Managers typically became managers by first having acquired skills as non-managers. Some of those skills can be refreshed and new ones added in placing former managers into new roles (e.g., team leaders, advisors, coaches, etc.).

But if push should ever come to shove, downsizing can be done humanely with managers and non-managers alike (i.e., in a positive manner through advance notice, counseling, outplacement assistance, and the like), and there is abundant guidance available on what to do right. [7]

Keeping Only Necessary Compartments

Any large corporation clearly needs some kind and degree of organizational structure, but it is essential not to over organize people and their work. Compartments like functional silos or departments (e.g., production, marketing, personnel, etc.) reflect too much organization and makes unity of purpose and effort impossible to achieve.

So compartments cannot be escaped entirely in any organization, and the idea of a "boundaryless" organization seems fanciful. [8] What is essential is that any boundaries must be permeable or porous. Consider the case of product design. Suppliers and important customers need to be "brought inside" for consultation, the first group on product parts the firm does not make, and the second group on what might be an ideal product and variations of it. Or consider a large corporation that breaks itself up into a large number of small business units. They need to be treated as an alliance or network of partnerships, not as separate and independent entities.

A starting point in minimizing compartmentalization might be to eliminate its miniature compartments called positions along with their titles and descriptions. Some 45 years ago a colleague and I wrote an article proposing that position descriptions be replaced by the documentation of performance expectations and appraisals. [9] It was several years later before it dawned on me that the time-honored practice of establishing positions should itself be eliminated and that "performance roles" should be "loosely" established instead.

What these roles are at any one time will depend primarily on three factors, how the work of the corporation is organized, opportunities and challenges impacting from the outside, and the capabilities of the empowered people in the roles. The best way to organize work so as to minimize compartmentalization is to eliminate all functional departments and reengineer the work into start-to-finish core processes that flow smoothly and naturally from beginning to end. They are referred to as "end-to-end" processes in the literature because they go from one end of the corporation's boundary, the one next to suppliers, to the other end that is next to external customers. But any process has to have a start and a finish or it is a meaningless tread mill activity.

There should be no more than three to four start-to-finish core processes (e.g., a build-to-order process or a process for new technology development) in a company or for each business unit within the company. [10] Since no one individual can or should work through a whole process alone, it needs to be done by teams of responsibly empowered people, preferably self-managed teams. Each team would be responsible for a particular phase in the process. Each team needs to have a team leader. Additionally, someone needs to ensure the whole process across the teams runs smoothly and meets expectations about its performance. That person is often called a "process owner," but I prefer the term "process leader" or "process captain" instead. Ownership by just one person is divisive. Everyone associated with the process anywhere along the way needs to have a sense of ownership and pride over it and its overall performance. Moreover, any vertical compartment turned into a horizontal one must not in reality be a chain of command and control laid down on its side!

A number of companies studied after they had eliminated unnecessary layers and compartments by organizing the work around core processes and creating self-managed teams to do the work were found to have achieved remarkable results. Nine managerial levels were reduced to three. Four to five months from order to delivery was shaved to three days. Output and operating margins doubled. Over a six-year period 170 new products were introduced, new markets were entered, and existing markets strengthened. Customer complaints about product quality dropped to near zero. Profits increased 20 percent. Earnings per share increased nearly three-fold over the six-year period while revenues per employee increased one and one-half times. [11]

Those results sound almost too good to be true, but I have no basis for doubting them. I do suppose though that there might have been other factors such as the status of the industry's market during the follow-up period that could have given the companies an extra boost.

Maintaining Structured Flexibility

I was conceiving the idea of structured flexibility at about the same time Tom Peters and Robert Waterman, Jr. were writing their book, In Search of Excellence. [12] They observed that the more successful companies they studied exercised rigid control while also insisting on and allowing employees to have autonomy, to exercise entrepreneurship, and to be innovative. They dubbed this practice the "loose-tight principle." But it is much tighter than structured flexibility because the use of rigid controls is inconsistent with the essential lowerarchy and the full empowerment of its people.

Structured flexibility means the right balance between too much and too little organization, between two much and too little procedures and their constraints, and between too much and too little policies and how restrictive they are. As for the relevance of the idea to organizational structure, retaining too many layers and too many compartments would be too much structure.

Enabling Corporate-Wide Empowering

There is absolutely no way for a hierarchy to enable corporate-wide genuine empowerment. The chain of command and control and all that goes with it stand in the way. Why is corporate-wide empowerment so critically important?

Corporate-Wide Empowerment
Eight Imperatives

The Biological Imperative
The Psychological Imperative

The Moral Imperative
The Medical Imperative
The Linguistic Imperative
The Physics Imperative
The Philosophical Imperative

The Biological Imperative

All species are genetically programmed to manage themselves and their own performance. Consider birds for example. [13] They manage to survive through different seasons. They manage to store food and remember where they stored it. They manage to find a mate. They manage to learn new songs. Now it stands to reason that since birds can successfully manage themselves around the clock, then mature human beings certainly should be able to do so, too, not just during the time they are away from their workplaces. While I am not implying that all people who work in un-empowering organizations are treated worse than birdbrains, it is not at all farfetched to say that such organizations are dehumanizing.

The Psychological Imperative

Empowerment is sound psychology. Numerous psychologists other than I have made this argument. I will mention just one of them. Recall in Chapter 2 Dr. Abraham Maslow's theory of human needs. [14] Ironically, it is a hierarchical theory, but in this case, a hierarchy of human needs that conflict with any organizational hierarchy. At the top of Dr. Maslow's hierarchy is the need to develop one's potential to the fullest, a need that can be met very nicely through being empowered.

The Moral Imperative

Empowerment is the morally right thing to do. Why is this so? Empowerment liberates people, and liberation is a "human obligation." [15] It is a human obligation because it upholds humanity's ethical values. Take, for example, the values of fairness, justice, and respect for others. Because power is more evenly distributed throughout the organization the abuse of concentrated power via unfairness, injustice, and disrespect is minimized if not eliminated.

Empowerment implies self-responsibility, which is another moral precept and necessity. Author Nathaniel Branden notes that "if we embrace self-responsibility---we commit ourselves to a profoundly important moral idea." [16] And responsibility is one of the universal ethical values.

I am going to let Michael Ventura, columnist and co-founder of the L.A. Weekly, have the last word on this particular imperative:

> *If the people who do the work don't own some part of the product, and don't have any power over what happens to their enterprise-they are being robbed. You are being robbed. And don't think for a minute that those who are robbing you don't know they are robbing you. They know how much they get from you and how little they give back. They are thieves. They are stealing your life.* [17]

The Medical Imperative

Numerous studies have shown that lack of a sense of self-control or of not being empowered increases stress levels and is bad for one's health in other ways. [18] As an extreme example of Theory X and worse in operation, consider this alleged exchange between the plaintiff's lawyer and a manager from an asbestos manufacturer:

> *Do you mean to tell me you would let them work until they dropped dead?*
> *Yes, we save a lot of money that way.* [19]

The Linguistic Imperative

Thinking, talking, and writing depend on language, and it can be a very powerful source of power. A Nobel prizewinner in literature, Toni Morrison, has noted an axiom we all know, namely, that words can be used to "sanction ignorance, preserve privilege, and create and perpetuate subjugation." [20] One of the meanings of subordinate, for instance, is that of being subservient in an inferior way. Or think of other authoritarian and subjugating terms obviously out of place in places full of empowered people, words like boss, order, direct, superior, supervisor, supervise, lines of authority, chain of command, and span of control.

The Physics Imperative

Newton's second law of physics tells us that for every action there is an equal reaction. The comparable law of hierarchies is that for every commanding and controlling action by management there is likely to be a counteraction by those managed. That basically has been the history of labor-management relations. Two British researchers studiously documented how workers, when they perceive they are being exploited by management, counter with work slowdowns, sabotage, and the like. [21] And the American scholar and business consultant, Dr. Edward Lawler III, has said that he is "regularly impressed with the ingenuity of the workforce when it comes to defeating management control systems." [22]

The Philosophical Imperative

One of the greatest modern philosophers, Immanuel Kant, regarded the autonomy of will as an intrinsic human condition. That is, you may force a person to act, but you can never will that person to act. We can only will ourselves. If you accept this as a logical premise, then it also follows logically that being empowered comes much closer to this intrinsic human condition than does being commanded and controlled by others. To Kant, there was nothing more dreadful than being subjected to the will of another. He surely would have endorsed the empowered version of the performance equation. The autonomy of will, incidentally, is also a logical prerequisite for accountability. A person without any other recourse who is forced to commit an action cannot justly be held accountable for it.

The Economics Imperative

There are numerous research studies that dramatically show the performance uplift from empowerment. In one study, for instance, the use of empowered teams led to immense payoffs such as 50% or more gains in productivity, 50% or more reductions in manufacturing costs, more work pride and more harmony throughout the organization. [23] In another study, a Fortune 500 company after reorganizing into self-managed teams was found to have achieved nearly

100 percent reduction in the number of production steps and also in the number of production errors. [24] Comparable results from many other studies and anecdotes could also be summarized here but it really should be obvious that empowered people can outperform commanded and controlled people.

A Caveat about Empowerment

Despite all of its imperatives, empowerment in any organized form comes with a big caveat. Empowering irresponsibly and being empowered without acting responsibly would be anarchy. It would be crazy, for example, to let thousands of empowered individuals run loose in the organization, all of the talk about "letting a thousand flowers bloom" not-withstanding. [25] This concern may underlie the argument sometimes made that the organization loses necessary control over what is happening if the organization's leader empowers everyone in the organization, particularly in the large corporation. But that argument is the old command-and-control mentality.

Two factors most crucial to whether empowerment will be responsible or irresponsible are corporate culture and performance management. They will be discussed in the next two chapters.

Summary

Tall and big corporations can never perform tall. They can only be what they are, the staple of the corpocracy that is ruining America.

CHAPTER 9
CULTIVATING AN UPLIFTING CULTURE

The culture of a company is like an autobiography that captures the very essence of the place, its history, its people with their shared beliefs and values, its rituals, its reputation, its formal and informal ways of operating internally and externally, and its outcomes. A culture, in other words, says "this is who we are, what we value, and how we do business."

Whatever its particulars may be, a company's culture usually affects for better or worse the company's internal operations and its financial performance. [1] Barbara Toffler, who, paradoxically-note this please, was partner-in-charge of the ethics program and responsible business practices at the now defunct Arthur Anderson firm, graphically tells about the wrong culture there in her insider's book, Final Accounting: Ambition, Greed, and the Fall of Arthur Anderson. She describes bosses who bullied, desperate sales pitches, excessive over billings, demeaning motivational hype, and a "brutally cutthroat" culture where "I learned to try to screw someone else before they screwed me." [2]

Allan Kennedy, who should know after co-authoring two books on the subject, says that "---as long as business needs people to function, people will build cultures---." [3] The question becomes then what kind of culture has already been built in an existing corporation and what is the best kind of culture for a corporation pursuing tall performance? If the existing culture has been one of anything goes, or screw or be screwed, raising that culture will require some heavy lifting.

The Essentials of an Uplifting Culture

Supportive Values
A Liberating Language
Organizational Justice
No Poppycock Rules
No "Officious Ethics"
Structured Flexibility*
Total Accountability*
*Next Chapter

Supportive Values

Communicating and cultivating values supportive of an uplifting culture has a head start given a top-level consensus that both positive success and positive failure will be valued, negative success and negative failure will not be valued, and all of the universal ethical values cited in Chapter 2 will be honored in practice throughout the corporation. Here are those values again:

The Universal Ethical Values
Honesty
Integrity
Loyalty
Promise Keeping
Fairness
Justice
Caring for and Respecting Others
Excellence
Responsibility
Accountability

Everywhere he looked in his search of recorded history, Michael Josephson, a lawyer turned ethicist-a novel career switch-kept finding these same ethical values. [4]

Two of them, accountability and excellence, may at first glance seem to be out of place. A little homework and reflection, however, suggests that Mr. Josephson is right on the mark. In the Holy Bible, for instance, both values are mentioned many times (e.g., "---we are in danger to be called in question for this day's uproar."; "---seek that ye may excel---"; "I shall show you a more excellent way."). That seems to give them ancient moral authenticity. Closing the bible, I then reasoned that accountability ought to be considered the guardian ethical value because adherence to it helps to protect the other ethical values. As for excellence, I reasoned that it is the sine qua non for quality, for as one corporate executive once remarked business is morally obligated to produce quality rather than shoddy goods and services. [5]

These ethical values reach across time. What was ethical in the beginning is basically what is ethical now. They reach across places and cultures. They reach across the broad spectrum of human endeavors. And they are independent of any religious beliefs, my bible not-withstanding. They are not to be confused with sectarian moral values or codes. They are humanity's ethical values.

They also provide a norm of behavior for interrelationships and transactions, exactly what make up the business world. There may not be any endeavor in business where ethics is irrelevant. The notion that business is amoral is sheer nonsense, a rationalization. I would be hard put to think of one business decision or action that does not have an ethical implication, directly or indirectly and whether small or large.

A Liberating Language

Language Can Make a Difference

From	To
Success	Positive or Negative Success
Failure	Positive or Negative Failure
Span of Control	Span of Responsibility
Authority	Responsibility
Bosses/Superiors	Words Abolished
Managers/Management	Performance Managers
Supervised	Responsibly Empowered
Rank and Status	Positive Achievement
Subordinates	Word Abolished
Labor/Workforce	Associates
Positions	Roles
Career Promotion	Role Diversification
Rules	Flexible Policies
Human Resources	People
Employee Relations	Camaraderie
Grievance Negotiations	Conflict Resolution

Recall the linguistic imperative for responsible empowerment. Cultural capital is diminished with each promoting or condoning thought and utterance of subjugating words, the oppressive and negative language of the hierarchy and tyranny in the workplace, a workplace sustained partly with the help of such language. Dropping the words on the left side of the above list and picking up the ones on the right would go no small way toward increasing tall cultural capital as long as, of course, the talk is also walked. Consider, for example, the traditional label "labor." It is a demeaning, "put-down" label. It is usually associated with organized labor or unions, a bête noir of the corpocracy.

Organizational Justice

The dictionary defines justice as a condition of moral rightness and fairness. This definition applies to justice generally and to organizations specifically. But the dictionary does not do justice to justice. Looking elsewhere, we find that there are five equally important conditions of organizational justice: procedural justice; distributive justice; interpersonal justice; informational justice; and retributive justice. [6] Where each applies in a given case, and usually they all do, the criteria of each must be met in order for there to be organizational justice. One-fourth to four-fourths justice will not do.

1. Procedural Justice

Procedural justice exists when the process used by the organization to make decisions are judged to be fair. A biased reward process, for example, would not be fair or just.

2. Distributive Justice

Distributive justice exists when the outcomes of an organization's decisions are judged to be fair. For example, does this condition exist when the CEO gets 400 times or more the compensation of people in the plant? I am sure the CEO's answer, at least the public one, is not the one the plant people give, at least privately.

3. Interpersonal Justice

Interpersonal justice exists when the manner in which people are treated throughout the process of making decisions affecting them is a positive one. For example, this condition would not exist if some people were treated disrespectfully inconsiderately in determining who would get rewarded.

4. Informational Justice

Informational justice exists when the information about the process and outcomes is fully available and when explanations about both are complete, timely, and clear. This condition would not exist, for example, if people were kept in the dark about the reward process and who got what rewards.

5. Retributive Justice

Faintly similar to distributive justice, retributive justice is "an eye for an eye" justice, so to speak. It is usually administered through formal penalties. Whenever organizational wrongdoing is not punished or is not punished sufficiently retributive justice is missing or is diminished. It also occurs in the form of grudges and retaliations against the organization by people who feel they have been exploited or unfairly treated in other ways. [7] Recall the physics imperative for empowerment.

A couple of points need to be made about these five conditions. They apply beyond the doors of the organization as well as within them. A business firm that decides to discharge its waste into a community's supply of drinking water, for example, is acting unjustly and certainly deserves a strong dose of retributive justice. Secondly, many times the judgments about whether any one condition has been met will be very subjective. But that is all right as long as the judgments themselves are not unjust. As the cliché says, "for justice to be done, it must also be seen as being done."

That organizational justice is a necessary and important part of a culture of greatness hardly needs explaining. The five conditions are not just musings. Whenever any one or more of the conditions is missing we have a case of organizational injustice, a version of wrongdoing that causes harm. People see and experience the injustice and that is why organizational justice matters to them.

How often injustice happens within corporations is obviously an impossible question to answer, but my guess is that it is a common occurrence especially within hierarchies. Numerous authors have documented in their books callous and abusive organizations and the myriad injustices against employee perpetrated by their employers. [8]

Examples of internal injustice include intimidating workers fearful of being downsized to work longer hours, boasting about employee assistance programs while minimizing the actual services provided, exempting workers to avoid paying them overtime, union busting, reneging on promises such as pension returns, allowing glaring inequities in compensation, applying double standards in sanctions, showing favoritism in performance appraisals, promotions, and other decisions and subsequent actions involving subordinates, sexually harassing workers, not allowing due process in disciplinary actions, and retaliating against whistleblowers.

No Poppycock Rules

"Poppycock rules," CEO Ricardo Semler wrote, "justify the worst silliness people can think up." So he got rid of all rules and instead encourages common sense, while acknowledging that it "is a riskier tactic because it requires personal responsibility." [9]

The corporate reform taskforce would have its hands full with this task. There must be a mountain of poppycock rules and inflexible policies in a large hierarchical corporation. The simplest and quickest way to proceed would be not to pour over any of them but instead to dump them all out and start from scratch. How many new policies will really be needed? My guess is very few. Common sense and the practice of structure flexibility ought to be the criteria.

No "Officious" Ethics

> *The ideal candidate will have significant and progressive experience in corporate business ethics, and be a strategic thinker committed to embedding ethics into all aspects of our business processes.*

This quote is an extract from a recruiting ad in 2006 on behalf of the world's largest retail corporation, Walmart, in its search for a "global ethics chief." [10] The ad appeared a year after the retailer's number two executive "admitted to stealing company money and goods." Some of the retailer's policies and practices were also causing its public image to be battered.

Does Walmart truly believe a "GEC" can "embed ethics

into all aspects of its business processes?" Not for one minute do I believe it. Moreover, a GEC and ethics program in any corporation may even make matters worse. I will explain my blunt view, starting with a true story about a defense contractor.

After allegedly repeated and egregious wrongdoing, the contractor finally got a directive from the government barring the company from further business orders until it established a compliance program. [11] The company quickly responded by retaining an ethics consulting firm to draft an ethics code, creating an ethics committee of outsiders to serve on the board of directors, hiring an outsider to be the corporate ethics program director, holding ethics workshops for employees, and opening a hotline for whistleblowers.

The ban was lifted in three months. The ethics program director was honored in a feature article of a professional journal in which he was quoted as advising companies to "do a few things very well because only a few things really need to be done." [12]

Well, not exactly, Mr. Ethics Program Director. I have been tracking publicity about the contractor for years following its heralded compliance program. There were reports about: low balling bids; violation of safety regulations; a bonus plan for the top 25 managers deemed "just outrageous" by a government official; giving a 10-year employee a layoff notice the very day the employee returned from bereavement leave following the death of the employee's young son; once named the "War Profiteer of the Month;" a recidivist defrauder of the government that gets slaps on the wrist and, of course, continued contracts; and its executives spin through the revolving doors of the military/industrial/political triumvirate like its one big cozy family. [13]

The contractor's compliance program apparently was nothing more than window dressing and undoubtedly gave the company a sense of impunity.

If not impunity when it comes to federal sentencing of the few corporate criminals who could not dodge the law, the US Sentencing Commission has obliged them by mitigating the sentence if the criminal's "culpability score" was low. Fines and other penalties are reduced up to 95% if the corporation's gets a low score by having adopted and begun implementing a compliance program prior to the offense. Now obviously the program failed or there would not have been an offense in the first place! The judge who chaired the commission declared that the provision for mitigation is a way to "reward organizations."[14] Does she really believe it? Not for a minute do I believe it. I believe the provision is a ludicrous example of a captive government at work.

But corporations are hell-bent to play the game, particularly after the corporate scandals of the Enron era ushered in "tougher" regulations. It has been a heady time for the "ethics industry." The Ethics Officer Association, a professional organization for GEC types trying to "embed ethics into all aspects of their corporate business processes," had 600 some members in 2000 and then doubled in membership only four years later. [15]

Corporations are also turning to a growing business of ethics consultants and suppliers in a "rush to learn ethics virtually overnight" and to adopt "cookie-cutter" programs. [16] One of the consulting companies in demand had helped to advise the U.S. Sentencing Commission on developing its requirements for corporate compliance programs and later had hired a TV script writer to be a "content author manager" directing a crew of writers of ethics and legal lessons. The writer reportedly "insisted" his previous experience was relevant. [17] Sure, tell that to any sensible person.

Besides ethics training, the typical elements of any ethics program include codes of ethics, hotlines, and provisions for penalties for transgressions. Each of these elements has serious drawbacks. Consider for a second each one. Ethics training, Socrates would remind us, is unnecessary, and no training regardless of how well done can ensure that what is learned will be used back at work. Codes of ethics are usually highly legalistic, often quickly "out-of-sight-out-of mind," and essentially worthless in that companies with codes do not do business any more or less ethically than companies without them (Enron was said to have had a "model" code). [18] The deterrence and corrective capability of hotlines is limited if they are seen as inconsequential or as a set up for retaliation when anonymity is not allowed-and allowing it can be criticized as an authorization of illegitimate concealment and as having "to hide in order to say anything of ethical consequence." [19] As for penalties, if scapegoats are unavailable, corporations are more likely to turn to a stable of lawyers to find loopholes through which to drive dubious defenses of CEOs and senior management.

It is absolutely impossible for any GEC and his or her program to "embed ethics into all aspects of the corporation's business processes." What is bound to happen instead is that ethics officers and their institutionalization of ethics will actually displace or diminish personal responsibility and accountability for ethical behavior, give the corporation a sense of impunity-or culpability that is easily afforded, and thus give the corporation the green light to continue business wrongdoing as usual.

The corporation may not be able to ditch its compliance program if it is a government contractor. But the corporation can do everything possible to streamline perfunctory "Officious Ethics" and mainstream real ethics into every day corporate behavior. The absolutely best way to do that is to mainstream ethics into the way performance is managed in the corporation, the subject of the next and last chapter.

The Role of the Culture Taskforce

The culture taskforce would decide how best to communicate corporate-wide news about the new corporate culture that is evolving and how best to cultivate and maintain the new culture aside from the rest of the implementation work to be done. One possibility would be to develop a loose leaf handbook for all corporate people entitled something like "The Pride of Our Company" or "Our Culture." In it could be sections presenting and discussing adoption of the Gold Standard, the corporate vision, and the like.

The culture taskforce has at least two important objectives in establishing and helping to maintain organizational justice. It must scrutinize all policies for how well or poorly they satisfy the five conditions of organizational justice. It must create better policies. It must establish certain critical means for ensuring organizational justice beyond mere policy. And it must, once it becomes an ongoing project group, help to maintain organizational justice. All of these objectives are straightforward save two; resolving conflicts and disputes, and handling whistle blowing and whistle blowers.

Resolving Conflicts and Disputes

Another useful part of the handbook should be a guide on conflict resolution. Conflict is inevitable in even the best of organizations, but not all conflict is undesirable. Conflict devoid of emotional, interpersonal wrangling can be creative and productive. What about potentially destructive conflict, on the other hand? The author of one book on the subject argues that interpersonal conflict can be avoided "almost entirely" if people within the organization treat each other as if they were important clients in a win-win rather than win-lose relationship. [20] Adopting that stance, of course, may sometimes be difficult to do.

So the author offers an approach he claims has been highly effective in settling interpersonal disputes. It is a multi-staged one in which any subsequent stage is only used if it has to be used. In the first stage, after acknowledging and setting aside their differences, the disputants search for a common ground in order to turn the conflict into a joint problem that can be solved collaboratively. If the first stage fails, the disputants continue, but use a different approach tailored to the stage reached at the moment. The dispute is either settled or a win-lose outcome is mutually accepted (there are many other sensible approaches to conflict resolution that could also be consulted). [21]

Handling Whistle Blowing and Whistleblowers

In a corporation headed toward tall performance there presumably would be no need to blow the whistle because there would be no corporate wrongdoing. Being realistic, however, the taskforce must absolutely not let this matter remain business as usual. Organizational justice would be blown to smithereens with just one typical handling of a whistleblower. [22] One possible approach would be to create a post of ombudsperson to hear any complaints and decide whether and how to proceed with the matter. [23] Whatever acceptable approach is taken, it must obviously meet all five conditions of organizational justice. Moreover, there is at least one issue that must be resolved, whether to allow the whistleblower anonymity or require disclosure of the person's identity.

An argument made for allowing anonymity is that it does not discourage people from blowing the whistle for fear of retaliation. Of course, in order to investigate an allegation there would need to be sufficient details about the incident under question, and those details would probably narrow the probable sources of the whistle blowing. It would seem that from the point of view of preserving "five-fifths" organizational justice disclosure ought to be required. One escape from this quandary might be to allow the whistle blower to have the choice, knowing that the choice will affect the type of response and very likely the outcome as well.

Monitoring Progress in Cultivating the New Culture

The taskforce would need to decide whether and how to monitor how well or how poorly the corporations is transitioning to the desired corporate culture. Measured monitoring, or guarded trust, would seem to be an appropriate option. This option is discussed in the next chapter.

Summary

Mention "corporate culture" to any typical corporate executive and expect to see the eyes roll upward. The culture is there, down trod-ding or uplifting whether it is confronted or not. It had better be confronted and changed for tall performance to have any chance at all.

CHAPTER 10
MANAGING THE WHOLE PERFORMANCE

Unmanaged performance is chaos, like a kindergarten class when the teacher leaves the room. So performance will almost always be managed and it can be done responsibly or irresponsibly. Irresponsibly managing performance always ends in it being short. Irresponsible or "short" performance management is the norm not only in the corporate world but in government as well. I ought to know. I spent much of my career studying performance management in large organizations, both corporations and government, and creating, perfecting, and applying new approaches to managing performance. [1] If I know one thing from A to Z, it is this subject.

Short Performance Management

There are four tell-tale signs of short performance management. When the first appears, the other three are sure to follow. The first is the setting of ignoble expectations at the very start. The other three that follow in succession are too much or too little monitoring, biased appraisals, and unconscionable rewards and penalties.

Ignoble Expectations

> *Hope of ill gain is the*
> *beginning of loss.*
>> Democritus-Greek philosopher
>> ca 450BC-ca370BC

The apotheosis of great expectations is ignoble expectations. The intent almost always is to maximize short-term gains or profits no matter how gotten. These expectations create "a corporate bulldozer that flattens every obstacle in its way." [2] Ethical considerations, of course, are the biggest obstacle. In one study comparing companies responsible for 25 of the largest frauds with 25 "fraud-free" companies, CEOs of the lawless companies were found to have set performance goals 250 percent higher and to have been rewarded stock-based pay eight times greater in value. [3]

The hierarchy is a hotbed for ignoble expectations, handed down by superiors, and by "superiors" I do not mean people of a superior ethical standing. As it cascades downwards, the silent or tacit message on the means to the ends is likely to turn into winks and nods before finally morphing into blunt orders to the doers at the bottom who must meet the expectations or else. Morality becomes situational, "and the situation is defined by your boss." [4] It obviously takes a stiff backbone to defy the message, as was the case of a manager who refused to fix prices. He was removed, and his successor was offered the position on the condition that the price fixing would resume. [5]

Too Much or Too Little Monitoring

In a corporate hierarchy the top monitors the bottom much more than the top monitors itself. Consider this true and disgusting vignette:

> The company installed a new monitoring system. The supervisor watches the computer screen, which records each worker's output the second it is produced. The company was quite pleased with the jump in productivity "despite amazing levels of demoralization and bad feeling. [6]

It is all guard and no trust at that prison of a workplace. The people there, though, at least knew that they were being hawked. According to a survey of Fortune 500 companies, many of them are never told. [7]

No amount of top-down monitoring, however, can ever tell the top all that it ought to know. It is just too far removed from the real work. Moreover, the bottom will tell the top only what it wants the top to know.

Self-monitoring at the top is typically nonexistent, starting with the board. An expert on governance noted a few years ago that "sleepy boards are commonplace all over the nation." [8] It is unlikely that they ever will fully awaken of their own volition. [9] As for CEOs and other originators of the ignoble expectation we can be sure they are looking the other way, all the while tacitly knowing what is going on and not disclosing it. Like mushrooms, corporate wrongdoing thrives best in the dark.

Biased Appraisals

Biased appraisals of performance whether of the corporation as a whole, of the CEO and senior management, or of everyone else give a distorted assessment of true performance and are not at all uncommon. The distortions are usually willful and meant to give more flattering assessments than unbiased appraisals would give so that rewards can be gotten and penalties avoided.

Biased appraisals of corporate performance go hand in glove with conventional accountability-call it rather, conventional unaccountability-of boards and CEOs for their performance, Flattering appraisals are made of financial performance, as witnessed in scandalous cases a la Enron.

Appraisals of corporate behavior either are not made or are also distorted. There is no appraisal of or any other form of corporate acknowledgment of negative successes or negative failures.

Biased appraisals are not new to modern-day corporations. Around the fourth century AD the Chinese philosopher Sin Yu complained that the Imperial Rater was showing favoritism in his ratings of the Royal Court's staff. [10] Anyone who has ever been rated in their lifetime by an imperialistic supervisor can empathize with Sin Yu.

Judging other people's performance is almost instinctive, and most people probably sense the need for performance appraisals. But what is aggravating and unjust is the irresponsible way they are done and by whom when it comes to the workforce. The appraising supervisor, the focus of the appraisal, and the appraisal procedure are all to blame. The supervisor, besides the stigma of being a supervisor, is unlikely to know enough about the subordinate's performance and very likely to give a biased appraisal regardless. The focus of appraisals is often on personality traits, an input, not an output. The appraisal procedure is usually a rating scale, and, like quarterly and yearly earnings' reports, is easily fudged. I once saw a rating distribution where 98 percent of the people were rated "outstanding." The only people who "stood out" were the few who did not get the fudged ratings!

All sorts of ill-advised schemes to prevent skewed rating distributions have been tried by management. The most ill-advised, although a favorite of Jack Welch, former CEO of GE, is the ranking of the workforce. [11] Rankings cannot compare the actual performance of each person against the initial expectations for that person's performance and consequently force arbitrary and unfair judgments to be made (the appraisals themselves, however, could be ranked, but only if the rankings consider performance-related information the appraisals themselves did not or could not take into account).

It is both galling and amusing that senior managers who think nothing of fudging financial reports and/or who think they are above being appraised themselves refuse to be dissuaded from foisting these schemes on supervisors who do the workforce appraisals.

Unconscionable, Upside-Down Rewards and Penalties

Oversize executive pay, back-dated stock options, insider trading, golden parachutes, rewards for negative successes and even for negative failures, impunity upstairs, draconian penalties downstairs, including penalties for positive failures are all what I mean by unconscionable, upside-down rewards and penalties. They pervade corporate America. [12]

The ratio of CEO to worker pay, sometimes 500-to-1 or more makes a mockery of organizational justice and the notion of pay for performance. How much should CEOs be paid? One CEO said not long after his excessive pay was spotlighted by Fortune that "nobody has any idea what the right level should be."[13] Not so, CEO. In his time, two millennia ago, Plato suggested a 9-to-1 ratio between the highest and lowest paid citizen. In his time, the late Peter Drucker suggested 20-to-1 between CEOs and the workforce. [14] Whatever the fair ratio is, the workforce ought to get far more and CEOs far less. If increases in stock prices are any indicator, what they indicate is primarily better economic and market sector conditions, not better CEO performance. [15]

Turning very briefly to unconscionable penalties, management is not prone to penalize itself. Punishment is largely reserved for the workforce. A particularly egregious example is management retaliation against whistleblowers, slowly crushing them in a succession of escalating actions diabolically planned to make the connection between the act of whistle blowing and the retaliation less obvious (the many laws supposedly protecting whistleblowers are mostly a sham). [16]

The Principles of Tall Performance Management

Total Accountability
Transparency
Self-Performance Management
Great Expectations
Flexible Monitoring
Valid Appraisals
Responsive/Responsible Rewards/Penalties

We have just seen how performance should not be managed but more often than not is. How it should be managed is guided by seven principles.

Total Accountability

Besides being the guardian of all universal ethical values, a minimum level of accountability is absolutely necessary for any business, or any society for that matter, to function. Achieving tall performance requires the maximum level, that of total accountability. For it to exist, both behavior and results must be managed diligently throughout each performance period or accountability cycle. The cycle must not be broken and must flow seamlessly into the next one. It must apply to every corporate member, no double standards allowed. Each cycle must start with great expectations about performance because they are the standard against which actual performance is compared. During the cycle performance must be monitored neither too much nor too little. At the close of the cycle performance must be validly appraised and, where appropriate or necessary, conscionably rewarded or penalized.

Because the immediate result of a decision or action may and is often intended to trigger a series of further actions by others, the question arises as to when the initial actor's accountability stops. The judge in the dumping case knew the answer. Along with power comes accountability for its use-at least in principle! It is violated every day in the corpocracy.

In any organization constructed as a network of partnerships accountability for results is shared but accountability for behavior ordinarily is not. If a team, for example, fails to meet one or more team objectives, the whole team is accountable for the shortfall. But a team cannot behave. Behavior is an action of an individual. Individuals are accountable for their actions as individuals. However, in cases where either tall or short behavior cannot be readily associated with any particular person, the whole team may need to be held accountable for the behavior (e.g., in the classical school room case where no one will tattle on the troublemaker).

Transparency

A turn up corporation will manage its performance in the "sunlight." This does not mean giving away proprietary secrets. It does mean not hiding any information detrimental to any stakeholders, including the environment. How can there be total accountability behind closed doors?

Self-Performance Management

Self-performance management is a hallmark of an essential lowerarchy. But there is the obvious caveat worth repeating. Self-performance management needs to be done responsibly and in a network of partnerships among corporate members whose performance is all headed in the same direction on the same journey.

Great Expectations

Proscribe Negative Behavior
Prescribe Positive Results

With apologies to Charles Dickens, behind every great performance is likely to have been a great expectation. When not a great one, it certainly could not have been an ignoble one! Great expectations, especially when self-owned so to speak motivate and guide people toward desired ends and not by using unacceptable means. Setting great expectations is critical, because a poor start usually ends poorly.

Proscribing rather than prescribing behavior may seem an odd corollary principle, but it is not. It says be flexible about positive behavior and inflexible about negative behavior. Incompetent, unmotivated, and unethical means, on the other hand, should never be tolerated. Expectations of positive results can often be met through a variety of positive means, each of which would be acceptable assuming there were no differences among them in terms of their cost and other considerations.

But the principle certainly does not preclude being less flexible or more structured about positive behavior when the nature of the work requires it. Obviously, there will be times when precise behavior, as in precision work, for instance, is critical and needs to be expected and to happen. Expecting positive results usually needs to be prescribed in very specific terms in the form of objectives that detail the quantity, the cost, the quality, and the deadline expected. Sometimes, though, as in the case of new product experimentation, the objective will need to allow greater latitude.

Flexible Monitoring

Three-fourths of the performance equation needs to be monitored in a principled way. Personal traits like intelligence or conscientiousness can only be "seen" through behavior. Saying that "people are monitored" is thus a misstatement. Their performance is what is being monitored.

Looking out for changes in internal and external conditions that could affect performance requires diligence. Bad changes overlooked or ignored can torpedo performance. Good ones missed are a lost opportunity.

All eyes need to be on the lookout for the possibility of badvantages. While the possibility of their existing is nearly nil within a corporation that is implementing the turn-up strategy, ethics can never be taken for granted anywhere. And although the behavior of the new corporation that is emerging ought to speak for itself, it may be advisable to augment the lookout with an occasional questionnaire survey that asks members their perceptions of any conditions that may favor unethical behavior.

An issue arises when it comes to monitoring the competition. Just how far can the corporation go? My answer is that it can go as far as possible as long as it does not fall below the bottom line of ethics. An example of how far without falling is the common practice of benchmarking a competitor's product by buying it and doing reverse engineering on it, although copycatting will never get a corporation to greatness. An obvious example of going too far would be industrial espionage, such as bugging a competitor's headquarters.

The monitoring of behavior needs to be in between too much and too little. Every person is responsible and irresponsible for countless behavior in their lifetime and hundreds if not thousands of minute to important acts each day on the job. Even heavy-handed watching of a fraction of worker action-inaction would amount to no productive work from the watchers.

Monitoring behavior, therefore, needs to be guided by the notion of guarded trust. It is the middle one of three levels of trust. The lowest is distrust, like the case I cited earlier in this chapter. The highest is unguarded trust, which may be too idealistic even for the most bonded marriages. In between is guarded trust. When there is tall behavior, lower the guard and rely more on self-monitoring. For behavior heading downward, raise the guard and also intervene. The practice of guarded trust is epitomized at a place like Semco where, for example, expense accounts on business trips are not audited. As its CEO, Ricardo Semler put it, "If we can't trust people with our money and their judgment, we sure as hell shouldn't be sending them overseas to do business in our name. [17]

Monitoring results requires every bit as much diligence as the monitoring of situations and involves keeping tabs on progress toward meeting objectives. Thus, progress indicators and reviews are needed along the way to ensure that performance is on target.

Valid Appraisals

Willfully distorting appraisals is an irresponsible and thus an unethical act which can have devastating consequences-recall the aftermath of the Enron scandal. Total accountability and the journey to tall performance require valid appraisals of both components of performance. A valid, summary appraisal basically gives an unvarnished, truthful answer to two questions: Were the expected results gotten? Were they gotten in a positive manner?

Responsive and Responsible Rewards and Penalties

The general principal to follow here is that if and when rewards and penalties are given they be given responsively and responsibly. That is, they must be given in response to the appraised performance and not also to extraneous considerations, and they must be given in a way consistent with the different meanings of success and failure and with the five conditions of organizational justice. The most irresponsible rewards and penalties would be ones that mock the standard of tall performance by rewarding negative successes and penalizing positive failures.

Years ago I developed policy suggestions to help steer organizations in their confronting the dozens of issues surrounding the giving of rewards and penalties. Some issues are relatively straightforward. Merit increases are an example. They should absolutely not be given because they are a continuous reward in the form of salary increments whereas the performance on which the increase is based is a time-limited occurrence. Giving performance bonuses to teams and their members, in contrast, is a thorny issue. For instance, if the corporation meets but does not surpass its year-end goals: a) should performance bonuses be awarded, assuming available funds; b) if bonuses are awarded should they be distributed equally among all of the teams; and c) should any MVPs (most valuable performers) be designated and given larger bonuses than their team members get?

My policy suggestions, some implemented, some not, provided workable answers to these and all other seemingly endless questions I have ever confronted in my research and consulting. Our model corporation needs to establish a corporate-wide taskforce to create policy guidelines and also performance review boards for each business unit to administer the overall monetary reward fund, to allocate a total amount for each eligible team, and to oversee the entire process, including the giving of any penalties.

How the Principles Might Work

The foregoing principals are far more important than is any particular approach that applies them. Nevertheless, I want to illustrate their application with two models, one for associates and the other for the board and corporate executives (the CEO, as few other central office executives as possible, and any business unit leaders). I have put the illustration in Appendix C because it is very detailed, and, as I just said, is less important than the principles meant to guide any particular application.

Summary

A turn up initiative requires that performance, not people, be managed. Performance is where the action is and its outcomes.

Performance is invariably mismanaged. If both parts of performance are not managed throughout the total accountability, forget about ever reaching the standard of tall performance,

PART THREE
CORPORATIONS AND CAPITALISM
LIFE WITHOUT THEM?

Let's brainstorm for a moment. Could Americans live without corporations, unreformed or reformed? Are any corporations really indispensable for meeting our really basic human needs as theorized by the psychologist, Abraham Maslow?

One industry probably indispensable in helping to meet several of our basic needs is the automobile industry. But due to a confluence of circumstances such as traffic congestion and diminishing fossil fuel the auto of tomorrow will be quite different both in its makeup and what it takes to make it and use it. Conceivably, there will be some day non-corporate makers of very different kinds of autos. It may not be too much of a stretch of imagination to conceive of cooperatives (see Chapter 10) making autos.

One thing is certain; there will never be life without corporations unless and until government stops favoring them.

Capitalism is another matter. In my opinion, socialism is not a viable alternative to capitalism. Government can't run itself very well and would do even worse as an automaker and what have you. That is why I look to different forms of capitalism in the last chapter, Chapter 11, for preferred options.

CHAPTER 11
SOME ALTERNATIVES
TO
CORPORATIONS

There are over six million business firms in the U.S. Only about 20% of them, almost all of them large are organized as corporations. Most of the others are self-employed persons operating unincorporated businesses and are hurt, not helped by the corpocracy.

While outnumbered 4 to 1 by all of the others, corporations make about 90% of the money and anyway they can. That's precisely why non-corporate forms of business need to be a vital component of America's marketplace. The less dependent on corporations Americans can become the less they will be subjugated and harmed by them and they will gain more control over their life equations.

While Americans have been conditioned by corporate America to want more than they need, to get it at the cheapest price, and to not ask about the hidden costs (costs like outsourced jobs, low wages, pitiful working conditions, pollution from byproducts, etc., etc.) a growing number of Americans want to deal as little as possible with corporate America whether on the producing end or the using end of goods and services. And that is why alternative forms of doing business are cropping up in America. This chapter explores some of them. In the next chapter we will consider some alternative forms of capitalism that are more hospitable and compatible with non-corporate America.

Some Alternatives

Cooperatives
Community Development Organizations
Community Land Trusts
Cutting Edge Ownership
Non-Governmental Organizations
Public Banks
Public Pensions

Cooperatives

Their distortion of Charles Darwin's classic Survival of the Fittest provides apologists with an excuse for the "anything goes" behavior of the "fittest" corporations. His research led him instead to conclude that "it is not the strongest of the species that survives, nor the most intelligent that survives. It is the one most adaptable to change." He also noted that a survival trait was the caring for each other and that "Those communities which included the greatest number of the most sympathetic members would flourish best, and rear the greatest number of offspring." [1] Mr. Darwin, I should think, would applaud the fact that there are now about 30,000 cooperatives in the U. S. They are mostly small enterprises, though. There are only 22 among the top 100 coops in the world. Their annual revenues range from 37.2 million to 3.2 million. [2]

According to the Center for Cooperatives "Cooperative organizations are organized to meet the common needs of a particular group of people." [3] The International Alliance of Cooperatives (ICA) defines a co-op as "an autonomous, voluntary association meeting common economic, social, and cultural needs through a jointly owned and democratically controlled enterprise." [4] There are several kinds of coops differentiated by the needs of their members.

Marketing coops (e.g., Land O'Lakes) are owned by and benefit members who use the cooperative to help sell their products. Consumer, purchasing and farm supply cooperatives (e.g., credit unions) are all organized to provide the specialized goods or services that their member patrons want to buy. Worker cooperatives, or employee-owned companies, are businesses that are owned and controlled by the workers (e.g., W.L. Gore). Multi-stakeholder cooperatives (e.g., Fifth Season Cooperative) are organized around a broadly defined goal that encompasses the specific interests of a combination of multiple member types. [5]

W.L. Gore, the maker of Gore-Tex Fabrics is a leader in its industry. Here is what the authors of "7 Cool Companies" have to say about it: "Employee ownership and a highly egalitarian workplace culture make W.L. Gore very different from your typical corporation. A worker may be a team leader on one project and follow others on another. Compensation is not determined by "the boss," but is tied to your contribution and decided by a committee, like many law firms. The firm regularly ranks on Fortune's "Best Companies to Work For" list." [6]

Cooperatives are certainly not a panacea. They have not replaced the corpocracy and never will by themselves. Their total impact on the U.S. economy about equals that of just one U.S. corporation; the largest, Walmart. Nevertheless, they offer alternatives to workers and consumers alike.

Community Development Organizations

Rather than corporate members of the corpocracy providing community redevelopment services at a price they can't afford and with inferior quality, there are some 5000 non-profit community development organizations in the U.S. that are revitalizing typically low-income, underserved neighborhoods or communities. [7]

Community Land Trusts

A community land trust (CLT) is a nonprofit organization that develops and oversees affordable housing, community gardens, civic buildings, commercial spaces and other community assets on behalf of a community. [8] CLTs, in other words, are a way to keep covetous corporations from privatizing with the help of their government pawn valuable resources that should belong to the public. There are currently over 250 CLTs in the United States. We shall revisit the subject of protecting the commons from predatory corporations in the next chapter.

Cutting Edge Ownership

In pure socialism I suppose no one individual would own any property. The state would. In the corpocracy's pure form of capitalism I suppose corporate America would own all property. In between are several different forms of ownership depending on what is owned and by whom or what. "Cutting edge ownership" is a catch-all term that refers to any nontraditional means of owning an enterprise for the common good. [9] A coop, for example, could thus be a cutting edge form of ownership.

Non-Governmental Organizations

Non-governmental organizations, or NGOs, may be funded by governments, foundations, businesses, or private persons. Some avoid formal funding altogether and are run primarily by volunteers.

NGOs are also a catch-all term for a heterogeneous group of non-corporate types of organizations engaged in a wide range of activities. Some are tax-exempt due to their non-profit, socially oriented status such as, for example, an antiwar or peace NGO. Some are front groups for political, religious or other interests. There are about 1.5 million NGOs in the U.S. [10]

From my research on nearly 200 NGOs I concluded that most of them seem to have been coopted by the corpocracy. The funding that these NGOs received could be considered "hush money" for not upsetting the status quo of the corpocracy. [11] If I am conclusion is valid, these NGOs, in other words, might as well be considered puppets of the corpocracy and as such are certainly not the desired kind of alternatives to corporations.

Public Banks

Does the following scheme make sense to you? Government has the power and authority to create and print money, but gives away that power to a private monopoly, the big banks, and then pays interest to borrow that money back? [12] Well, it obviously makes beaucoup dollar sense to the banking industry. That is why the Vermont Banking Association, the private banks' lobbyist group, fought very hard to thwart the creation of a public bank in that state.

Apparently the bankers' lobbyists were not as powerful in North Dakota. It, alone, in the US has a public banking system. Furthermore, it is outperforming its private counterparts. The reasons why are a no-brainer. According to Ellen Brown, lawyer, author, and President of the Public Banking Institute, the North Dakota public bank has substantially lower costs and risks; has no exorbitantly-paid executives; pays no bonuses, fees, or commissions; has no private shareholders; and has low borrowing costs; does not need to advertise for depositors (it has a captive deposit base in the state itself) or for borrowers (it is a wholesome wholesale bank that partners with local banks that have located borrowers); has no losses from derivative trades gone wrong; engages in old-fashioned conservative banking; and does not speculate in derivatives. [13]

Don't expect many if any other states to follow suit until the banking industry's ally, the government, stops being an ally.

Public Pensions

The last on my list, public pensions, is a benefit promised and honored by all levels of government agencies to their public employees. Not so with their counterparts, hapless employees of corporations. These soulless entities "have been freezing pensions, slashing retiree health benefits and eliminating 401(k) contributions." [14]

To include public pensions on a list of alternatives to corporatism is an alternative only if corporate employees become government employees. And that alternative seems to be a shaky one as state and local governments particularly are experiencing underfunded pension plans. [15]

Summary

Corporations with government in tow exploit rather than meet the basic needs of humanity. This chapter has explored some alternative ways humanity has organized itself to meet its basic needs. While they ae a long way off from replacing mighty corporate America they are a chink in its armor.

CHAPTER 12
SOCIALLY RESPONSIBLE CAPITALISM NOT SOCIALISM

America's form of capitalism is the corpocracy's form of capitalism, an arrangement aided by government for making and selling products and services that gives corporate America an immense badvantage over general public America. America's form of capitalism is predatory and a bankroller of war.

At the opposite end of the spectrum of economic systems is socialism, the control of the market by government. Socialism is definitely not an acceptable alternative. Government doesn't run itself well. How can we expect it to run our economy? The best government is doing now is helping to ruin our economy.

The espousal of an uncontrolled or free market by Adam Smith, the putative father of capitalism, has been far overblown. He made only a passing reference to "the invisible hand" in his Wealth of Nations and never once in it used the term "capitalism." [1] A moral philosopher, he understood the importance of morality, which he believed was manifested in a person's sympathy for others. He would have recoiled at the very idea of the corpocracy and its capitalism, for Smith thought the emerging corporations of his time posed threats emanating from their unlimited life span; unlimited size; unlimited power; and unlimited license. [2] Look familiar don't they?

Alternative Capitalism

Not wanting to throw out the baby with the bath water, let's take a brief look at some alternative forms of capitalism, six of them to be exact. [3] Not one of their authors is an economist. Why? Nearly the entire economics profession was blindsided by "Economic Katrina," my name for economic hurricane of 2008 that drowned Main Street.

Peter Barne's Capitalism 3.0

Peter Barnes co-founder, president, and director of various socially responsible businesses, wants "capitalism 3.0" to replace "capitalism 2.0," the existing economic "operating system." [4] He complains that corporations, with no resistance from our government, are privatizing the commons, profiting from it and externalizing the costs.

He defines "the commons" as assets we all share by inheriting or creating them together and subdivides them into three sectors, nature, community, and culture. Together they represent our "common wealth" (a most insightful concept), in contrast to our "private wealth," the latter representing all the property we inherit or accumulate individually.

Private wealth collectively in the U.S. was estimated to be around $48.5 trillion in 2005. What do you think our total American common wealth is? Economists can't begin to estimate it in its entirety, but what they can estimate, Barnes tells us, comes to about $70 trillion. Is it any wonder then why, as Barnes asks, corporations on the one hand take valuable stuff "worth trillions of dollars" from the commons for short-term profit and on the other hand dump bad stuff into nature's commons and pay nothing? Corporate America, moreover, drools over the prospect of privatizing ever more chunks of our common wealth.

His proposal relies heavily on the idea of property rights because our U.S. Constitution guarantees them, they shape economies, they produce value or wealth, and, most importantly, there's no requirement that they be concentrated in profit-maximizing hands, thus opening up the possibility of "propertizing" the commons without privatizing it (another very insightful idea). He proposes that the government assign common property rights to institutions, distinct from government and corporations that would be set up as trusts to manage the common property (recall the previous chapter). A few such trusts already exist in the U.S, such as a trust in Marin County, California where ranchers can sell easements to it. For natural assets with their limited sources, the institutions would need to be capable of limiting their use. For the other two sectors with their endless potential, public access would need to be maximized and public usage fees minimized.

He introduces the idea of "commons tax credits" as a means for funneling more money into trusts by raising taxes in the uppermost tax bracket and giving its wealthy taxpayers the choice either to pay the extra tax to the government or to one or more qualified trust funds.

Barnes adapts the economist's concept of rent, or money paid because of scarcity, to his proposed trusts for nature. The trusts would sell pollution rights to polluters and get the rent in return. The trusts would limit the number of rights sold so as to increase the cost of their rent. For corporate polluters the cost would be high enough to create an incentive to pollute less. Some of the rent would be converted into per-capita dividends for consumer citizens. Consumers of pollution-laden products would pay more in rent (via higher prices) than they get back in dividends, while consumers of less-polluting products would get back more in dividends than they pay in rent. It is in this way that rent gets recycled from over-users, who tend to be the wealthier ones to under-users, who tend to be the poorer ones. This shifting of income would help alleviate what Barnes calls a pathological flaw of capitalism 2.0, the wide income gap between high and low income groups.

Barnes also shows how there could be per-capita dividends from trusts created for the commons' other two sectors. For example, treating the capital market as common property, a trust could charge a usage fee to publicly traded corporations for selling stocks and for having been given various rights such as limited liability, perpetual life, copyrights, patents, and the like.

Over time the propertizing of the commons would amass a portfolio worth trillions of dollars that could be used to fund three "universal birthrights;" a regular dividend to everyone, an opportunity endowment for each new child, and health insurance for everyone. Clearly, Barnes' proposal is a very expansive one and, superficially at least, a seductive one. Barnes appeals to capitalists, wage earners, lawyers, economists, commons entrepreneurs, and others to help build the commons sector into a full-fledged capitalism 3.0 and shows how it can benefit each of these diverse groups.

His proposals are among the most unique I've ever read on capitalism. His advocacy of pollution rights, though, really troubled me until I got a further explanation from him. I was troubled because to me every human being has a sacred obligation to nature and a moral obligation to generations yet unborn to respect nature, not a right to pollute.

When I mentioned to Barnes my concern he explained that his proposal is a market-based one that doesn't imply moral approval of pollution. [5] In contrast, giving rights away free would imply some moral or social approval. But the rights would not be free with his approach. They would have to be paid for, and the money paid (i.e., rent) would benefit everyone. Furthermore, the rights would not be permanent, but would be for one time only. He also reminded me of his assertion in his book that "It is more disrespectful of the sky to pollute it without limit or payment than to turn it into a common property held in trust for future generations." [6] Moreover, he continued, every human being is a polluter and pollution can't be stopped over- night. So the best we can do, he says, is to steadily reduce our polluting. And to do that requires, as he has pointed out, a declining quantity of pollution rights with rising prices and per capita dividends. This internalizes the external costs of pollution and creates the virtuous recycling from over-users to under-users.

Gary Brumback's Peoples' Capitalism

I have slipped myself into this alphabetic list of authors and their versions of alternative capitalism because I'm not an economist and I also authored an alternative version of capitalism. It's a chapter in my book, The Devil's Marriage. [7] The chapter, Ending Undemocratic Capitalism, and an accompanying appendix that summarizes the views of the other authors on my list here are very long, so I will only highlight my treatment of the subject.

In that chapter, after overviewing how exploitative both domestic and global capitalism is, I set the stage for true economic reform by proposing a taskforce commissioned by some nongovernmental group and charged with polling the opinions of middle class Americans, the socioeconomic group absolutely essential to any true democracy and viable economy, and then melding the solicited public opinion with the taskforce's a) consideration of new ways of

128

thinking about capitalism; b) enunciation of a proposed new national economic policy; c) design of a new form of capitalism that I'll simply refer to as the "people's capitalism," d) proposed objectives and initiatives to implement the design, and e) report on the findings and recommendations to the administration, to the Congress, and to the American people (I referred to the new form of capitalism as "democratic capitalism" in The Devil's Marriage).

I then proposed in detail ways to end the worst features of the corpocracy's undemocratic capitalism; namely, free market ballyhoo; fear mongering over national debt; privatization; economic disparities and poverty; shut-out capitalists; financial speculation; exploitative globalization; unsustainable development and elitist pay without performance.

For each of those features I explained why it must be ended. For example, in proposing that the stock market be phased out over time while protecting long-term investors until the process is completed, I explained that much of the stock market is a cesspool of investments in socially irresponsible corporations; that there just aren't that many socially responsible corporations beyond their window dressing in which to invest; that; those corporations that invest only for making money rather than for product and service improvements are no longer truly useful or necessary for the real marketplace of goods and services; and finally, that start-ups can go to local banks rather than through initial public offerings.

Riane Eisler's Partnership Capitalism

Riane Eisler, trained in sociology, anthropology, and law, wrote a book about the "real wealth of nations." Unlike

Adam Smith's classic work, "the wealth of nations," which monetizes wealth and focuses on the market, Eisler argues that the real wealth of a nation ultimately depends not on the market but on the quality of its human and natural capital. [8] Yet it is this very capital that the corpocracy exploits for its own self-interests to the detriment of what she believes ought to be the primary purpose of any economic system, the promotion of human welfare and happiness. The economy, in other words, should not exist solely for corporations or even for the marketplace.

From her perspective, neither corporations nor the marketplace are at the center of any viable economic system. The center, she says, is the household economy because it is there that the socially and economically essential work of caring for people and the development of future contributors to economic productivity start. This household economy, therefore, needs to be given the most attention in economic reforms. They would include, for instance, recognizing the household as the core economy, placing a monetary value on the work of care giving, accounting for its positive contribution to productivity in economic indicators such as the GDP, fairly compensating care givers, and making massive investments in child care and human development programs.

Her perspective is so broad that she adds five more economic sectors to that of the core, household sector. They are the unpaid economy made up mostly of volunteers; the conventional market economy; the illegal economy like illegal arms trade; the government economy that includes not just the large population of government workers but also the laws, rules, and policies that (should) govern the market economy; and the natural economy, a sector as basic as the first in that our environment produces natural resources used and misused by the market economy.

A functional economic system along with its larger context would be one she posits that depends on what she calls the partnership model of mutually respectful and caring relations as opposed to the traditional and current domination model. She shows how the Nordic countries, the only ones coming close to her partnership model, are faring well economically and socially. Having a national capacity and resources for providing optimal human development is clearly necessary for having a healthy economy, and she persuasively links the domination form of child rearing and thus suboptimal human development to adverse consequences later in life that show up in the kinds of leaders and followers our society has, in our belligerent relationships with other countries, and in our diminished capacity for a functional and healthy economy. She also argues convincingly how disastrous it could be if the domination model is played out with new and risky technological developments on the horizon.

She makes a number of practical suggestions about what needs to be done on Wall Street (e.g. stiff taxes on short-term speculations), in government (e.g., massive investment in child care and human development), by business leaders (e.g., changing from top-down to empowering corporations), and among social activist citizens (e.g., mounting a global movement to change laws and customs-she describes how she wrote an amicus brief that helped women legally gain equal rights).

Jeff Gate's Shared Capitalism

Jeffrey Gates wrote a book jam packed with ideas about what he calls "shared capitalism for the twenty-first century." [9] His is a decidedly populist view, not surprising since he was counsel to the U.S. Senate Finance Committee (1980-87), working with Senator Russell Long of Louisiana, son of populist governor and U.S. Senator Huey P. Long. In this role, Gates crafted federal law on employee stock ownership plans (ESOPs) and pension plans.

Capitalism creates financial capital, not capitalists, he notes. Moreover, most financial capital is held by institutional investors, the absentee owners of public corporations. This, he says, creates a "detached and disconnected capitalism largely on automatic" with investment decisions devoid of longer-term concerns, including the costs of externalization.

Unshared capitalism, while made to order by the corpocracy, is totally unfit for a democracy. His solution is to make widespread ownership a specific goal of national economic policy.

Achieving inclusive ownership on a national scale will take, he believes, a political era like the progressives and populists of the 1930s and a leader like FDR. Gates identifies six strategic initiatives: a public opinion poll that asks the right questions about inclusive ownership and informs politicians about the public will, which he believes would support populist capitalism; a government declaration of widespread ownership as a national economic goal; a bipartisan commission on economic empowerment, which he believes will conclude the desirability of widespread prosperity; a government office of asset ownership; a regular assessment of what the impact of inclusive ownership has been; and an annual ownership survey to determine who owns what.

Hawkins, Lovins, & Lovins on Natural Capitalism

These authors of a book of the same title warn that if we continue to ignore the value of natural capital, i.e., nature's life-support systems for humankind, there will come a time when there won't be any more life support. [10] Doomsday may be a century or two away, but the quality of life up to that point will have deteriorated at an increasing pace.

Pursuing four central strategies of natural capitalism, these authors say, will enable commercial enterprises and communities to operate as if all forms of capital were important. The core strategy is that of radically increasing resource productivity by being more efficient, less wasteful in how natural resources are extracted and used. The second they call "biomimicry" that involves eliminating waste in the making of things by imitating biological processes in the manufacturing process. The third is to change the relationship between producer and consumer from one based on goods and purchases to one based on a "flow of economic services" that will in turn deemphasize possession as a measure of affluence and emphasize that well-being depends on the "continuous receipt of quality, utility, and performance." The fourth involves "reinvesting in sustaining, restoring, and expanding stocks of natural capital."

Roger Terry's Nation of Owners

Roger Terry wrote a book in 1995 on "economic insanity" (no, it isn't a "mis"fortune telling of the insane meltdown of 2008 thirteen years later). [11] He's co-founder of a small business firm, the "fun company."

Terry contends the growth-driven capitalism of big, authoritarian, and unaccountable organizations is devouring the American dream. As proof he points to the erosion of the good life of being happy; how we have become a nation not of citizens but of consumers of "life-style enhancing" things, yet in actuality we produce more (in waste) than we consume in products and services; how seeking limitless economic progress is both illusory and self-destructive; how we live in a capitalistic society, but most of us are dependent wage earners, not independent capitalists; and how the rich are getting richer and the poor are getting poorer-an inevitable result of capitalism.

Terry questions three underlying and inherently false assumptions of our current capitalistic system; 1) limitless, perpetual economic growth is an imperative good, 2) increasing productivity is a cure-all for an ailing economy, and 3) maintaining a good life depends on continuous technological advances.

The growth imperative, he argues, is illogical, immoral, misguiding, and destructive. It's illogical because we consumers buy products we don't really need (e.g., personal computer upgrades) from companies that are fearful of not making and selling new products lest their competitors do so and grab more of the market share. It's immoral because it lets companies rationalize wrongdoing for the sake of survival. It's misguiding because companies are diverted from what should be their true purpose, to serve society in useful ways. It's destructive because our planet and our pocketbooks are being irretrievably depleted by a growth-driven, consumer-oriented economy.

134

He argues that productivity increases, contrary to the prevailing assumption, don't make the economy grow and thereby don't improve our standard of living. He observes that while productivity has gone up over the last 25 years, real wages haven't. Productivity increases, instead, are siphoned into the pockets of the rich, into pay for support people (e.g., consultants) who don't produce anything, and into payments on un-forgivingly huge debts fueled by the growth imperative.

Technological advances, he claims, are "inherently self-destructive" because they are "quickly bankrupting us." Only a few select companies and the more affluent among us can afford the technology race. The rest go out of business or into deeper debt.

He goes on to outline the features of a new economic system. It would be a structurally different capitalism, one we've never seen before. It would be a "Nation of Owners," in which there are three levels of ownership: (a) small enterprises, like his own, with the founders and a few partners who share ownership commensurate with their seniority and other factors like start-up funding; (b) larger enterprises, the corporations of today, would be owned collectively by their members, who would elect managers for limited terms of office; and (c) public enterprises, such as utilities, education, defense, and the like, would be created and managed by public boards or local governments.

Here is a sketch of what he says life would be like under this different capitalism. It would be a "truer form" of capitalism because anyone able-bodied and "even minimally motivated would own capital and in reasonably equal portions," thus guaranteeing freedom of opportunity and markedly reducing inequality of income. There would no longer be a Wall Street since absentee owners, i.e., shareholders, would gradually be replaced by working owners, which in turn would eliminate the motive of short-term profits and its immoral consequences. Our government would be much different-it wouldn't be controlled by a corpocracy. Our economy would be developing better rather than growing bigger. Businesses would be motivated to serve society instead of serving themselves. There would be no more drudgery at work, exploitation of workers, cutthroat competition, takeovers, downsizings, wholesale firings, ballooning personal and collective debt, frivolous products, superfluous support structures, or any other ills you might associate with the present system. Sounds like utopia, doesn't it?—unless you're a fat-cat CEO or you can't wait for the next computer upgrade.

Summary

The corpocracy's capitalism must be ended. Socialism is not the answer. Six alternative forms of capitalism are presented. Each, or some amalgamation of the six, would be the answer.

EPILOGUE

Where Do You Stand
And
Where Are You Going?

If you are a diehard member of America's corpocracy you know where you stand, over the trash where you dumped this book if somehow it got in your hands. But please retrieve it and give it a second thought.

If you are an enlightened, open-minded, and influential member of a corporation or one of its stakeholders become a champion of the turn up initiative.

If you are a business consultant, advise your clients about the possibility and desirability of a turn up initiative.

If you teach about business tell your students about the ideas in this book.

If you think corporations are due their reckoning help make it happen.

If you are a social entrepreneur see how you might apply this book.

If you are worried about the future of America become a social activist or an even more active one.

APPENDIX A
CORPORATE WRONGDOING
EXAMPLES

Controlling Life's Equations

Over Our Personal, Social, and Cultural Spheres

Ceaselessly promotes materialism and consumption.
Dominates and manipulates the mass media.
Spews propaganda, half truths, and zero truths.
Prevents truly universal, more aflordable health care.
Commercializes and privatizes education.
Trains our youth as vigilantes.
Commercializes religion.
Invades our privacy.
Callously forecloses on our homes.
Uproots homes for commercial development.

Over Our Economic Sphere

Prevents the people's general welfare.
Loots the people's treasury.
Over taxes the many, under taxes the few.
Wrecks havoc with the American economy.
Profits from Economic Katrina.
Creates unconscionable income inequality.
Creates spiraling levels of unemployment.
Provides only substandard wages.
Outsources work and takes it off shore.
Emasculates worker unions.
Creates monopolies and Big Box stores.
Causes the collapse of small business firms.

Abandons communities in bad times.
Advertises falsely.
Gouges consumers with excessive prices.
Creates unsafe/unhealthy products.
Privatizes and manipulates scarce resources.
Manipulates international trade agreements.
Commercially exploits poor nations.
Privatizes and degrades public utilities.
Starves and privatizes social services.
Excessively promotes consumerism.
Devours and bankrupts honorable companies.
Escapes accountability for lawlessness.

Over Our Political Sphere

Hijacks our Constitution.
Buys politicians.
Dominates Supreme Court rulings.
Hand picks judges.
Erects voter hurdles.
Lobbies intensely for its own special interests.
Installs special interest office holders.
Always trumps public interests with corporate interests.
Controls laws and regulations.
Stonewalls government investigations.
Scams state and local governments for subsidies.
Promotes and profits from U.S. militarism.
Privatizes the military.
Privatizes law enforcement.
Weakens true security in breeding dissent.

Over Our Environmental Sphere
Treats natural resources as commodities and waste dumps.
Pursues unsustainable development.

Collusion with Government

Acting unlawfully and expecting and getting no or negligible accountability
Bribing legislators with campaign money
Collaborating with government in the war and spy business
Lavishing legislators with perks
Persuading legislators to enact laws favorable to corporations
Persuading regulators to minimize, eliminate, or overlook enforcement
Persuading legislators to authorize unnecessary expenditures
Seeking and getting handouts
Seeking and getting unconstitutional Constitutional rights

Collusion with Other Corporations

Fixing prices
Rigging bids
Carving up markets

Exploiting Local Governments

Exploiting Local Governments and Communities
Extorting state and local governments for subsidies
Abandoning local communities after exploiting them

Exploiting and Harming Customers

Advertising falsely or deceptively
Knowingly selling hazardous, defective and substandard products and services
Limiting access to services

Over pricing
Red lining

Exploiting and Harming Workers

Allowing dangerous and unhealthy working conditions
Cutting back or reneging on benefits
Demanding excessive work pace and output
Demanding right to work laws
Fighting labor unions tooth and nail
Firing workers without due cause
Outsourcing jobs
Paying substandard wages
Persecuting whistleblowers
Requiring unpaid overtime work

Exploiting and Harming the Environment

Plundering finite resources
Polluting the environment
Hartman, host of the nationally syndicated radio program
Air America and prolific author, argues convincingly that
the "corporatocracy," his term for the corporate aristocracy
that seeks to control all aspects of our lives, is "screwing,"
his term again, the middle class through such means as
demonizing labor unions and shrinking them by shifting
more and more jobs overseas, lowering wages through
government sponsored free-trade, getting the government
to shift more and more wealth upwards, and to deregulate
everything in sight having to do with commerce.

APPENDIX B
AMERICA'S SADTISTICS

Corporate America dictates to government America
Endless wars and other military interventions
Excessive deterioration of public infrastructures
Expelled from the U.N. Human Rights Commission
Frequent domestic gun violence and fatalities
Gangs (over 1 million)
Government's disregard for international accords/treaties
Government's failure to promote the common welfare
Government's inhibition of dissent
Government lawlessness and unaccountability
Government's surveillance of all citizens Government's use of torture
Half of public school students live in poverty
Huge income inequality
High unemployment rate
High rate of overall poverty
Large population of homeless
Large prison population
Lost domestic opportunities from a $1trillion national security budget
Low life expectancy
Militarized and homicidal police
Millions of financial hardships from medical bills
Millions of foreclosed homes
Millions of American livelihoods dependent on warring and spying
Privatization of public services
Racial hatred and violence
Six deaths a day from lack of health insurance
Surprising but not unexpected blowbacks

APPENDIX C
TALL PERFORMANCE MANAGEMENT

Applying the Principles
Two Illustrations

Presented here are two models for a turn up initiative, one for associates and the other for the board and corporate executives (the CEO, the few other central office executives, and the business unit leaders). The associate's model is presented first because doing so is symbolic of a "topsy-turvy" lowerarchy-the once last are now more like the once first so to speak, and because the board/executive model is derived from the other.

The Associates' Model

Setting Great Expectations

The general scheme of both models for setting great expectations is that results are prescribed in the form of specific objectives while all short behaviors are proscribed in the form of generic examples. Throughout the corporation every partnership group (e.g., the teams throughout each business unit) sets "We" expectations, and every individual member sets "Me" expectations through an interactive and iterative process. No more handing down ignoble expectations from the top through layers of management.

This process allows self-performance management to be done responsibly in that expectations are always cross-checked for alignment with the expectations within and across the relevant partnerships, whether parallel, upstream, downstream, or within a group. The "grand" expectation is that by meeting all of the "We" and "Me" expectations corporate-wide the corporation will advance on its journey to tall performance.

In applying the model, the We, or team, objectives, are set first. This is done in an interactive and iterative process with the executive team.

Once all team objectives are set, team member objectives are set. Team and team member objectives differ in several respects. Because their accomplishment contributes to broader goals, team objectives are broader. Because they are broader and because there are fewer teams than individuals in the organization, there will be fewer team objectives. Finally, team objectives will target end results such as products to be delivered or services to be provided, whereas individual objectives will mostly target intermediate or enabling results such as process improvement outcomes or components of the product or service that contribute to the end result.

After confirming their respective roles and responsibilities team members draft their individual objectives and action plans that will contribute to the team's objectives. The team meets again to review and ratify each member's objectives and action plans before going into action.

Unlike objectives, which need to be revisited and reset each year, behavioral proscriptions once established seldom need to be changed (changes in core competencies might require changing "core in-competencies"). The corporate-wide taskforce on performance management creates the proscriptions by developing generic examples of incompetent, unmotivated, and unethical behavior for publication and company-wide distribution. Accounting for whether wrongdoing has indeed been avoided is thus mainstreamed into a vital process, the accountability cycle. There is no code of ethics to be sidelined and forgotten.

Monitoring Performance

Under normal circumstances, self-monitoring of team member behavior is sufficient. But if any short behavior begins to surface, monitoring and intervention by other team members would be required. More structure and less flexible monitoring is needed to monitor progress toward meeting objectives, not out of any sense of distrust, but simply because objectives are too important to leave anything to chance and/or to any changes in situational circumstances (e.g., an unexpected announcement or a new product by a competitor). Daily dashboard-type monitoring should be done. The analogy is not perfect-looking through the windshield is still critically necessary along the way and verifies that the destination has been reached. The value of dashboard "gauges" is to give each team intermediate indicators (e.g., status of suppliers' deliveries) of its progress toward performance targets. [1] These indicators enable teams to make just-in-time adjustments whenever needed before they are too late to make.

Appraising Performance

The solution "over 2000 years in the waiting" for appraising individual and team performance I have argued is to combine self-appraisals (no supervisors anymore), yes/no questions (no ratings or rankings anymore), and a complete focus (no personality traits anymore). [2]

Allowing self-answers to appraisal questions may seem like a hair-brained scheme but it can work and for several reasons. First, it would take a bald-faced lie, not a fudge, to answer "Yes" when the truth is "No." Second, answers to questions about results are readily verifiable. For answers to more sensitive and subjective questions about behavior, there are built-in safeguards such as verification by others and an evidentiary trail in cases where the guard had been raised and interventions undertaken. Third, when enough of the right questions are asked, yes/no answers are sufficient for validly differentiating performance where true differences do indeed exist and are sufficient for making decisions (e.g., bonus awards) based on the answers. Fourth, performance is usually on view in the "glass-house" of a team-based organization. Fifth, penalizing falsified answers makes the falsifying too risky.

At the end of the performance period, self-appraisals would be made by answering a series of about 20 yes/no questions first about individual performance and then about team performance. The two sets of questions are similar and are given in some of my earlier writings. [3] Here is a small sample: "All objectives met?" "Which ones if any were exceeded and what were the extra gains?" "Any unexpected and very tough obstacles encountered?" "Manner of performance consistently positive (if not, briefly describe what happened if not already documented)?" "Any positive or negative feedback received from other teams, customers, vendors?" "Two corporate people outside your team who know your performance well?" "Nominate anyone as an MVP (Most Valuable Performer)?"

Some questions are necessary in order to make determinations about performance-sensitive bonuses (if the performance management taskforce endorses the use of them). Only asking if all objectives were achieved and if manner of performance were consistently positive would not allow for any further differentiation of performance. All individuals and all teams, after all, are expected to meet their objectives and to do so in a positive manner. But favorable answers to certain of the questions ought to warrant a bonus consideration.

If two people concur with the self-appraisal, they recommend team certification of it. If one or neither concurs they review all relevant documentation (such as, e.g., any positive/negative feedback or any attempts to rescue falling performance) and then try to reach a consensus. If none is reached, the appraisal is forwarded to the team for resolution.

Each team then appraises its own team performance. Someone outside the team who knows the team's performance relatively well (identified in the team's self-appraisal) should be invited to attend this second meeting to reinforce objectivity. The team appraises its team performance by answering questions essentially comparable in content and purpose to the questions about individual member performance, including those intended to help the business unit's performance review board (PRB) determine whether any teams should receive a larger share of the company's performance bonus pool. To underscore the interdependence of all the teams and their link to overall corporate goals, each team is asked if any other teams contributed to their team's accomplishments, and conversely, if their team contributed to any other teams' accomplishments.

Next, teams send their self-appraisals of team performance, any unresolved appraisals of individual performance, and all accompanying documentation (e.g., data on team results) to the PRB. It may change or leave unchanged any appraisal before certifying it. Any changes made in team appraisals may require revisiting member appraisals to see if any changes also need to be made in one or more of them.

Rewarding Performance

The corporation's performance management taskforce should decide in favor of bonuses as the primary reward option and against merit pay increases and then should create guidelines for awarding bonuses (later in this Appendix).

Once the status of all appraisals has been determined, the PRB decides whether none, some, or all teams deserve bonus shares and whether any differences in performance justify larger shares. The PRB comes to this decision after putting the appraisals of team performance into qualitatively different categories.

The first two categories would be for teams in which all members' manner of performance was consistently positive and all objectives were met. But the first category would be reserved for any teams with patterns of appraisal answers that demonstrated even taller performance (MVT or Most Valuable Teams). Any teams in this first category would get larger shares. Most of the teams would presumably be in the second category and would get smaller shares.

A third category would be for any cases of positive failure where all members' manner of performance was consistently positive, but one or more objectives were not met. Whether any still smaller shares are awarded to teams in this category would depend on the specifics of each particular case and on whether the remainder of the bonus fund would allow meaningful shares.

A fourth and final category would be for any cases of negative success or negative failure. No team in this last category should be considered for a bonus share unless the shortfalls in behavior were those of one or more team members having had absolutely no role in the objective(s) involved. Such an exception is advisable because it is possible to have short performance from one or more team members and still meet and even exceed the team objectives in question.

Once a team has received its bonus share, monies from it can be allocated among the members according to whatever rationale the team chooses consistent with the guidelines. For example, the team could emulate the PRB's procedure and put its members' appraisals into comparable categories and then decide on bonus allocations among and within the eligible categories. The team could also decide to set aside some of the money for use by the whole team.

Penalizing Performance

Another guide (later in this Appendix) to be created by the performance management taskforce together with the organizational culture taskforce is one on punishable behavior. Using the guide minimizes arbitrariness and yet allows for mitigating circumstances to be considered. The guide is in two parts. The first gives examples of punishable behavior. The second assigns a level of harmfulness or costliness to each example, considerations more important than the frequency of the behavior. A minor infraction can happen several times and never reach the level of harmfulness of an extremely serious one. Three levels of harmfulness/costliness are sufficient; less serious, more serious, and illegal. For illegal offenses, obviously, legal authorities will weigh in with their own determinations. To determine the level for a given incident, questions like those listed in this Appendix need to be answered. Note that only the last two questions relate to frequency of the offensive behavior. The rest relate to the nature of the behavior's consequences.

Once each level is operationally defined by examples, suggested penalties need to be listed for that level. Penalties for the most harmful/costly level should be considered first. It is helpful to ask in considering a specific penalty if it would be perceived as being reasonably less than penalties for offenses at a more serious level and reasonably more than penalties for offenses at a less serious level.

Punishing its own members is probably the most difficult task a team ever has to face. But it must do it anyway for three reasons. A team, being fully empowered, should not shirk any of its responsibilities. Second, the team is in the best position to penalize its wayward members (in the true spirit of empowerment, a person could be allowed to suggest his or her own penalty). They know each other's performance better than anybody else. And by solving their problems of short performance, I believe they strengthen, not weaken, themselves through the experience. Third, while difficult, the task is not an impossible one. Teams have the guide to follow and they can seek advice from the PRB.

Any individual or team facing the prospect of punishment may seek to nullify or reduce it by appealing to an independent hearing board. Due process is quasi-judicial and requires a careful balancing of structure and flexibility for the sake of fairness and justice. To keep flexibility within reasonable bounds, the same due process should be followed through the company. The process needs to be as streamlined as possible and reserved for only the more serious offenses and harsher penalties.

The Executive Team Model

Tall performance management needs to be done seamlessly and similarly throughout the corporation and that includes its executive team (e.g., CEO and business unit leaders). The associates' model can be used almost like a template for this team at the (lower) top.

Setting Great Expectations

In preparation for the new performance year the steering council would initiate an iterative exchange among all corporate teams, starting with a year-end meeting of the board and the executive team. Year-end performance appraisals of the corporation as a whole and of each business unit are reviewed and certified once any disagreements are reconciled, with the council acting as an arbitrator. Unit leaders present drafts of unit goals that reflect what the teams think their team objectives should be for the new year.

An umbrella plan for the corporation is then drafted of corporate and business unit goals, including any new strategic initiatives, and then submitted to the council. It reviews the plan against various criteria (e.g., whether all objectives and their performance targets are aligned with corporate and unit goals, whether interdependencies required among teams and/or other business units have been accommodated, etc.) and has the final authority to ratify the plan except for strategic initiatives that require board concurrence. Once the plan is ratified, We objectives are set by the board and executives as a partnership team. Objectives derive from the plan and the responsibilities and roles of the members of the team.

Members of the executive team share accountability for the corporation's and the units' performance equations respectfully. That is a whale load of accountability, but "if you can't stand the heat, get out of the kitchen," as I believe the late President Truman put it. Objectives for the executive team, therefore, should be targeted toward optimizing the equations so that tall inputs are in place and maintained and, on the output side, wrongdoing is being shunned and further progress toward greatness is being made. For example, one of the team's objectives during implementation of the turn-up strategy would/should be to ensure that the corporation has been restructured into an essential lowerarchy as planned and scheduled.

Besides targeting outcomes of the turn-up initiative, the objectives should routinely target performance measures like those of the "balanced scorecard" developed by an accounting professor and a business consultant. [4] Their scorecard provides answers to four questions: "How do we look to shareholders?" "How do customers see us?" "What must we excel at?" "Can we continue to improve and create value?" I would recommend broadening the second question to include other stakeholders, expand the fourth question to include multi-faceted wealth, and add two more questions: "Are we shunning wrongdoing?" and "Where are we on our journey to tall performance this cycle?"

Before the executives' team and individual team member objectives are ratified, two overriding questions should be asked and answered about each: How exactly will meeting it contribute positively to the corporation's and business units' performance equations and to the balanced scorecard as modified? Can the objectives be met ethically?

The same principle of proscribing short behavior also applies to this model. A search for examples of short behavior by CEOs and unit leaders ought to be a short but productive search! The examples could be provided by the performance management taskforce with input from the board and executives. There should be behavioral expectations or proscriptions for such considerations as the way in which the turn-up initiative are handled, the way in which decisions are made, conflicts handled, and performance managed.

Monitoring Performance

No more sleepy boards! Several board members should be official "Corporate Monitors" with responsibility for getting periodic reports from say, the council, the executive team, and the performance management taskforce on the condition of each component of the corporation's performance equation and the condition of each component of the balanced scorecard as modified throughout the performance year so that critical questions can be answered during board meetings.

The questions ought to be about the manner in which business is being conducted, whether achievement of results is on track, and on any problematical changes happening or anticipated in situational and people factors. The data should also include the dashboard type of measures previously mentioned.

Progress reviews should be held on a regular basis and when emergencies arise. The executive team would monitor their own performance and add the information to that already gathered.

Common sense and guarded trust ought to prevail in determining just how much monitoring is just right under the circumstances. An example of excess beyond reason or need in my opinion is the case of the CEO of the world's biggest steel maker who required plant managers to submit over 60 monthly reports detailing every penny of costs. [5]

Appraising Performance

The appraisal of corporate and business unit performance should be made by comparing it against expectations about two major and big variables, the performance equations and the balanced scorecard as modified. The corporate overseers should be responsible for designing with the help of the performance management taskforce all of the quantitative and qualitative measures of those two variables.

Some of the measures like financial ones will be quantitative and tend to dominate traditional appraisals. But if financial accounting scandals have taught us anything it is that guarded trust, if not downright distrust, needs to be exercised in accepting at face value objective measures, most especially the financial ones. Objective measures are more vulnerable to gaming, more short-term, and more inconclusive; whereas subjective measures can be more comprehensive and conclusive.

Different financial measures give very different assessments of a corporation's financial health. One director of stock market research, for example, derides the standard accounting measures such as earnings per share as being in the eye of the beholder and easily fudged and prefers instead to use a host of measures to assess the corporation's return above its cost of capital. [6] Whatever financial measures are used they need to covey accurately the total financial component (including the monetary costs of wrongdoing and other externalized consequences) of multifaceted wealth.

Assessing performance directed toward maintaining and improving the four components of the corporate performance equation (personal and situational inputs, behavior and results) by necessity will require developing and using some qualitative and thus more subjective measures. But not everything worth appraising is countable and thus such measures need to be developed and used because without them a complete and valid appraisal is not possible. This is certainly true in appraising the manner in which the corporation does its business (as reflected, of course, in the behavior of the corporation's people). It is also true for assessing excellence in services rendered and products made, bought, and used. To be sure, proxy measures can be used as indirect and partial indicators of even the more highly subjective attributes of performance (e.g., defect rates as an indicator of quality).

The executive team appraisals would use the question and answer format along with having safeguards for doing the self-appraisals. Recall, for example, the questions asked in using the balanced scorecard. For each member of the executive team the overarching question that must be answered is: "To what extent and how did you contribute toward the corporation's progress toward reaching our goals this year?"

The process for doing the appraisals should be done in a way that neither undermines collegiality and cooperation nor compromises the journey to tall performnce. There are many possible approaches. For example, the CEO could prepare a self-appraisal and give to the rest of the executive team and the board, and they in turn would appraise the CEO's performance or provide feedback on the self-appraisal. A similar process could be followed for self-appraisals of the rest of the executive team.

Rewarding and Penalizing Performance

The priority concern should be to avoid even the appearance of unconscionable, upside down rewards and penalties for members of the executive team. The guidelines are merely a starting point for a committee on executive compensation to develop specific policies-better still in this case-less flexible but not poppycock rules!

The business literature is awash with commentaries and recommendations about executive compensation. To give you just two examples, there are nearly 40 recommendations made in a scholarly paper by two business professors, and Fortune recently issued "Five Commandments for Paying the Boss." [7] The committee needs to have the performance management taskforce scour that literature and summarize the recommendations concerning the various components of board and executive compensation (e.g., base pay, cash incentives, equity-based incentives, etc.). Personally, I agree with the writer of a letter to Business Week who argued that executives earn their bonuses in "cold, hard cash based on [meeting] specific performance criteria for the year." [8] As for the level of CEO pay, surely if a value can be calculated for an entire corporation, one can be done for CEO pay. [9] And if the board, in seeking a new CEO, is not looking for a celebrity but instead has carefully screened candidates, then the new CEO should have no problem accepting the recommendations of the compensation committee.

The committee should prepare several alternatives, including one submitted by the CEO, and perhaps one submitted by the largest shareholders. The total dollar value of each alternative should be divided into two components, a range for non-variable or base pay and a range for

156

variable, or performance dependent pay. The latter would constitute the reward aspect of total compensation.

The alternatives ought to then have to face some common-sense questions before a final decision is made. [10] Are we talking stupid money? That is, would only a stupid person offer such stupendous compensation? Who gets first dibs? The CEO probably contributed a minor portion of the corporation's multi-faceted wealth for the year ending. Maybe the corporation should get first dibs by investing much of the money in long-term initiatives. What's really a fair share? The answer of one CEO cited in the "Executive Pay Hall of Shame" was "fourteen times the pay of the average employee."[11] Now that is getting a bit closer to Plato and Drucker's ideal ratios. It could conceivably be even less in a real lowerarchy of empowered teams where only the very biggest decisions affecting the entire corporation are heavily influenced by the CEO, and/or where, as Peter Drucker advocated years ago, the CEO ought to be just one member of an executive team. [12] Does it pass the gut check? There is a saying in jurisprudence that "the thing speaks for itself" when the transgression is so egregious that there is simply no defense for it. And finally, If the CEOs of the S & P 500 were in a contest to see who would and could work effectively for far less pay, what would that amount be? If it would be far less, then they are vastly overpaid.

Turning to compensation of board members, there are two major choices, stock options and direct ownership. The well-known consultant and prolific author Edward Lawler argues that "the right choice seems clear." Every board member should be a direct and substantial owner by being compensated in shares. [13]

157

The use of penalties for unacceptable performance by members of the executive team should be decided by these people after consulting with the performance management taskforce and then put into policy at the beginning of a performance year. The use of penalties should be guided by the same considerations that apply to the associates, should be the same for all executives rather than being tied to contracts unique to whomever happens to be the executive at the moment, and obviously should not contain ridiculous stipulations like forbidding dismissal for "bad judgment" or "negligence." [14]

We have come to the end of my sketches of two models for managing performance tall. The two exist nowhere in corporate America, and, that is one good reason why corporations fall far short of tall performance.

But there are still two more sets of guidelines to go, one on rewarding performance, the other on penalizing performance. Both apply to either the associate or executive model.

More Guidelines for Responsibly Rewarding Performance

For rewards to be an incentive for tall performance several additional guidelines need to be followed.

Rewards in General

1. Preserve Organizational Justice. All conditions of organizational justice need to be satisfied in rewarding performance.

2, Make Rewards Targeted and Valued. Rewards need to be targeted and valued and targeted. Poorly targeted awards where the performance that should be wanted is not the performance rewarded must be avoided. The value of the rewards needs to be commensurate with the value to the corporation of the performance. Both trivial and excessive rewards will be counterproductive.

3. Customize Rewards. People value different rewards differently. The clear implication is that people should have a say in how they are rewarded and compensated. Where there is empowerment, customization of rewards is probably is inevitable.

4. Reward Positive Failures when Justified. Not only should positive failures never be penalized, rewards of some amount should be considered for taking risks that fails despite ingenuity and prodigious effort by the risk takers.

5. Do Not Tolerate, Let Alone Reward, Negative Successes. Rewarding or even tolerating ill begotten success is an unethical practice and begets more ill begotten successes. These successes need to be penalized instead. Sounds idealistic, yes, but it does happen occasionally (an example is cited in discussing the principles covering penalties).

6. Think Twice before Rewarding Ethical Behavior. It is debatable whether rewards should be given for ethical behavior. It is an obligatory act in a corporation seeking greatness. What is not debatable is that ethical behavior must never be penalized.

7. Do Not Reward with Merit Pay. Giving pay raises to reward performance should never, ever be used. Pay is salary, not a reward for performance during a particular year. Pay raises are very cost ineffective. They are rarely if ever withdrawn when there is a drop in performance the

next year. So the raise lives on to death as an annuity. Moreover, when a conventional rating is fudged upwards by a supervisor to favor a subordinate (as often happens), the pay raise becomes a gift that keeps on giving.

8. Reward Teams and Individuals. Both team members and the team itself need to be eligible for monetary rewards (unless there is a consensus to the contrary). There is always the possibility that the tallest performance of one member is what makes the team excel, and everyone on the team knows it. Not to reward this MVP (most valued performer) is to risk alienating or losing him or her, but giving the MVP substantially more money or not rewarding the (positively) successful team at all sows dissension among the rest of its members. [15]

9. Be Open about Rewards. Hierarchies are usually very secretive about who gets what. Secrecy, an accessory to power, breeds mistrust and discontent. People need to see that there are no unconscionable rewards.

Bonuses in Particular

1. Bonuses may not be available if the company's annual goals aren't met.

2. All teams and individuals may be eligible for bonuses.

3. "We" will be put before "Me" in bonus considerations.

4. Consensus will be sought in decisions about bonuses.

5. All decisions will be documented and openly available.

6. Due process will be made available for proposed penalties.

7. The PRB will allocate bonus shares to the teams.

8. The teams will allocate their bonus shares internally.

9. Any MVPs and MVTs will be eligible for meaningfully larger bonuses.

10. Only positive successes and positive failures will be eligible for bonuses.

11. Anyone may exchange bonus eligibility for equivalent compensation.

12. Neither trivial nor extravagant bonuses will be awarded.

13. Ethical behavior may be rewarded but only if exemplary.

14. Bar stock options.

Penalizing the Wrong Behavior

For penalties to be a disincentive, that is, a deterrent and punishment for unacceptable behavior these additional guidelines need to be followed.

1. Preserve Organizational Justice. All conditions of organizational justice need to be satisfied in penalizing performance.

2. Penalize Unmotivated and Unethical Behavior Only. Incompetent behavior should not be penalized. Mastering the knowledge and skill needed are usually the solution for incompetence. If not, dismissal may be necessary, but it is not punishment.

3. Penalize Sooner than Later. Due process to allow for either verification or exoneration should not be unduly long. Justice delayed is justice denied. In the same light, waiting until after the year-end appraisal to account for punishable behaviors occurring much earlier obviously is an avoidable delay. When this is allowed to happen, the punishable behavior will snowball and also erode respect for organizational justice.

4. Penalize Publicly. Punishment must be publicized, but responsibly so. The adage, "for justice to be done, it must be seen as done," has double meaning. People who know about the offensive behavior but do not know about the unpublished punishment will tend to think the punishment did not happen or was too lenient. And the knowledge that punishment will be published is itself intended to be a deterrent to others.

5. Avoid Upside-Down Penalties. Worth repeating, ethical behavior in particular and positive failure in general must never be punished. Every time they are wrongdoing is given a badvantage.

6. Penalize Individuals, Maybe Teams, Too. Penalties ordinarily do not apply to teams because individuals are the source of behavior. A team with no members would be an abstraction without action. Team penalties should only be considered on the rare occasions where it is impossible to single out the irresponsible individuals.

7. Fit the Penalty to the Offense. Punishment must fit the offense. Because lenient penalties may encourage more offenses, the link between penalties and offenses should be relatively tight, but not so tight as to turn into a lock

because each case needs to be considered in terms of its own circumstances.

The performance management taskforce needs to develop more specific guidance for fitting penalties to the offense. It needs to include examples of punishable behaviors and recommended penalties for the different examples.

Before appropriate penalties can be suggested, the level of harmfulness or costliness of the behavioral examples needs to be estimated. This is a much more important consideration in choosing appropriate penalties than is the frequency of the offensive behavior. A frequently repeated minor infraction can never reach the level of harmfulness of an extremely grave infraction. Nevertheless, frequency obviously shouldn't be ignored or tolerated if it becomes a real issue.

Three levels of harmfulness/costliness ought to be sufficient to help determine the appropriate penalty; namely, less serious, more serious, and illegal. The first two cover both wrong-do and won't do behaviors. For illegal offenses, obviously, legal authorities will weigh in with their own determinations.

Here are some questions the elaborated answers to which will help differentiate among the three levels:

- What was the actual behavior?
- Which if any ethical values breeched?
- Was a law violated?
- Exactly what harm done or cost incurred?
- Who and how many people/organizations harmed?
- Financial, physical, psychological nature of harm ?
- Company's reputation jeopardized or tarnished?
- Customers/suppliers alienated/lost?

- Media attention?
- Monetary value of harm/cost can be estimated?
- Remedy available to undo harm/cost?
- Cost to organization of remedy?
- Remorsefulness shown?
- Offer to help on a remedy?
- Recurring behavior and response to it?
- How likely is the behavior to recur?

Note that only the last two questions relate to frequency of the offensive behavior. The rest relate to the nature of the behavior's consequences.

Flagged examples from a handbook or actual incidents can be used as a frame of reference in defining the different levels by tying answers to them. For example, "fighting on the premises" might be labeled "legal/less serious;" whereas lobbying Congress might be labeled "legal/serious." The definitions can be refined in any subsequent revisions of the guide as experiences with them accumulate.

Once the levels are operationally defined, suggested penalties need to be listed for each level. The kinds of penalties available need to be brainstormed first. Then, different penalties need to be recommended for each level of harmfulness/cost. Penalties for the most harmful/costly level should be considered first. For example, dismissal ought to be suggested for the most serious legal and illegal offenses (but, of course, with actual dismissal awaiting the outcome of due process if it's invoked). Then penalties for lesser offenses should be considered. It's helpful to ask in considering a specific penalty for a given level of offenses whether the penalty would be perceived as being reasonably less than penalties for offenses at a more serious level and reasonably more than penalties for offenses at a less serious level.

NOTES

Preface

1. Brumback, GB. The Devil's Marriage: Break Up the Corpocracy or Leave Democracy in the Lurch. Author House, 2011.

2. Bakan, J. The Corporation: The Pathological Pursuit of Profit and Power. The Free Press, 2004.

Part One. The Age of America's Corpocracy: How Much Longer?

1. Brumback, GB. The Devil's Marriage: Break Up the Corpocracy or Leave Democracy in the Lurch. Author House, 2011.

2. Figures compiled from Center for Responsive Politics, OpenSecrets.org.

Chapter 1. Government Hands Off and Handouts

1. Nace, T. Gangs of America: The Rise of Corporate Power and the Disabling of Democracy. Berrett-Koehler, 2003, p. 74-75.

2. Estes, R. Tyranny of the Bottom Line: Why Corporations Make Good People do Bad Things. Berrett-Koehler, 1996, p. 47.

3. Nace 2003, op. cit., p. 79.

4. Brumback, GB. America's Oldest Professions: Warring and Spying. Create Space, 2015,

5. Ibid., Appendix A.

6. Thiele, E. Military Spending: Cost of Iraq War is but the Tip of the Iceberg. Global Research Online, June 14, 2010, www.globalresearch.ca.

7. Brumback, GB. The Devil's Marriage: Break up the Corpocracy or Leave Democracy in the Lurch. Author House, 2011.

8. Strachan, M. These 26 Companies Pay No Federal Income Tax. The Huffington Post: Business, February 26, 2014.

9. Dixon, K. Corporate Tax Breaks Cost U.S. Government $180 Billion Per Year: GAO Report. Reuters, June 15, 2013.

10. Quigley, B. Ten Examples of Welfare for the Rich and Corporations. Common Dreams, January 13, 2014.

11. Story, L. As Companies Seek Tax Deals, Governments Pay High Price. The New York Times, December 1, 2012.

12. Kiel, P. & Nguyen, D. The State of the Bailout. ProPublica, April. 20, 2015.

13. Fisher, D. Chrysler Might Have Done Better Without Bailout, Study Says. Forbes, October 19, 2012.

14. See www.lockheedmartin.com; also, Hartung, W.D. Is Lockheed Martin Shadowing You? How a Giant Weapons Maker Became the New Big Brother. TomDispatch.com, January 11, 2011.

15. See, e.g., Gabel, M. & Bruner, H. Globalinc. An Atlas of The Multinational Corporation. The New Press, 2003; and, The Economist. The Biggest Transnational Companies. The Economist Online, July 10, 2012.

Chapter 2. Anything Goes---Until

1. Nace, T. Gangs of America: The Rise of Corporate Power and the Disabling of Democracy. Berrett-Koehler, 2003.

2. Josephson, M. Teaching ethical decision-making and principled reasoning. Ethics: Easier Said than Done, 1988, (1), 27-33. Mr. Josephson, found these universal moral values from his search of history and different cultures.

3. Zellner, W., et al. Everyone Loved Enron. Business Week, December 17, 2001.

4. Asmus, P. 100 Best Corporate Citizens: Companies that Serve a Variety of Stakeholders Well. Business Ethics, 2004, 18, (1), 4-12; see also, Labaton, S. S.E.C. Says Fannie Mae Violated Accounting Rules. New York Times.com. December 16, 2004.

5. Klinger, S. Harmful Enron Practices Widespread: Awards to Most Enron-Like Companies; GE is No. 1. www.faireconomy.org/press/2002/titans-pr.htlm, 2002.

6. Brumback, GB. When the Ivory Tower is Toppled by Reality: The Case of Corporate Social Responsibility Research. Industrial and Organizational Psychology: Perspectives on Science and Practice. Vol. 6, Issue 4, December, 2013, 387-390.

7. Brumback, GB. Corporations and the Gold Standard. Palm Coast, FL: Democracy Power Press (Kindle Edition).

8. Maslow, A. Motivation and Personality. Harper and Row Publishers, 1970. See also, Maslow, A. Toward a Psychology of Being. Wiley and Sons, 1999.

9. See, e.g., Brown, E. Monsanto, the TPP, and Global Food Dominance. OpEdNews, November 27, 2013.

10. Todhunter, C. Genetic Engineering and the GMO Industry: Corporate Hijacking of Food and Agriculture. Global Research, January 3, 2012.

11. See, e.g., Brumback, GB. Inside the corpocracy: Big pharma and big government. Cyrano's Journal, June 18; Dissident Voice, June 18; and OpEdNews.com, June 21, 2013; and also, Adams, M. Big Pharma Criminality No Longer a Conspiracy Theory: Bribery, Fraud, Price Fixing Now a Matter of Public Record. Natural News, July 9, 2012.

12. Brumback, Ibid.

13. Wolfe, S. Worst Pills, Best Pills: A Consumer's Guide to Preventing Drug-Induced Death. Pocket, 2009.

14. Lustgarten, A. Poisoning the Well: How the Feds Let Industry Pollute the Nation's Underground Water Supply. Cyrano's Journal, December 31, 2012.

15. Giambrone, J. The Most Fascistic Industry. Opednews.com, March 16, 2012.

16. Political Economy Research Institute. Toxic 100 Air Polluters. August 2011; see also, Boyce, JK & Ash, M. The

Toxic 100: Top Corporate Air Polluters Identified. Political Economy Research Institute, August 17, 2012.

17. Kampa, M. & Castanas, E. Human Health Effects of Air Pollution. Environmental Pollution
Vol. 151, Issue 2, January 2008, Pp. 362–367.

18. Goldenberg, S. Just 90 Companies Caused Two-Thirds of Man-Made Global Warming Emissions. The Guardian, November 20, 2013.

19. Gerken, J. 11 Animals That Are Now Extinct ... And It's Our Fault. The Huffington Post, October 23, 2013.

20. National Science Foundation. Ecosystem Effects of Biodiversity Loss Rival Climate Change and Pollution. Science Daily, May 2, 2012.

21. Nace, op. cit., p. 1.

22. Mokhiber, R. Top 100 Corporate Criminals of the Decade. Corporate Crimereporter.

23. Smith, A. U.S. Trucking Industry Corruption. Ask the Trucker, January 10, 2010.

24. Wrage, A. Shipping is "Most Corrupt Industry." Port Technology, April 22, 2015.

25. Nader, R. Unsafe at Any Speed. Grossman, 1965.

26. Carpenter, Z. Ralph Nader on the GM Scandal: "Detroit has Washington Pretty Greased." The Nation, April 1, 2014.

27.	Brumback, GB. America's Oldest Professions: Warring and Spying. Create Space, 2015,

28. www.brainyquotes.com Note: While this is a widely cited quote the Archives and Library staff of the Henry Ford Benson Ford Research Center could not verify its authenticity.

29. Rivero, M. All Wars are Bankers' Wars! What Really Happened. January 14, 2013 Radio Show. www.whatreallyhappened.com

30. Brumback, 2015 op. cit., Chapter 8.

31. Kimball, D. Nuclear Weapons: Who Has What at a Glance. Arms Control Association, June 23, 2014.

32. Boyle, FA. American Militarism Threatening To Set Off World War III. OpEdNews, December, 12, 2012. See also: "Chossudovsky, M. Towards a World War III Scenario: The Dangers of Nuclear War. E-Book Series No. 1.0, Global Research Publishers, 2011; and Roberts, PC. Pushing Toward the Final War. OpEdNews, March 28, 2014.

33. Turse, N. America's Secret War in 134 Countries. The Nation, January 16, 2014.

34. Brumback, GB. Op.Cit. pp. 223-227; see also, Nader, R. Smarter Foreign Policies or Bigger Blowbacks? Ralph Nader Newsletter, July 10, 2015.

35. Nader, R. Unstoppable: The Emerging Left-Right Alliance to Dismantle the Corporate State. Nation Books, 2014.

Part Two. Corporate Self Reform: The Turn Up Initiative

1. Brumback, GB. The Devil's Marriage: Break up the Corpocracy or Leave Democracy in the Lurch. Author House, 2011; and Brumback, GB. America's Oldest Professions: Warring and Spying. Create Space, 2015.

2. Brumback, GB. Corporations and the Gold Standard. Palm Coast, FL: Democracy Power Press (Kindle Edition), 2010; and Brumback, GB. The Corpocracy and Megaliio's Turn Up Strategy. Palm Coast, FL: Democracy Power Press (Kindle Edition), 2012.

Chapter 3. Some Fundamentals

1. Roland, N. & Mathewson, J. Sunbeam Ex-CEO 'Chainsaw Al' Dunlap Settles SEC Case. Bloomberg News, September 4, 2002.

2. Surowiecki, J. Back to Basics. The New Yorker, May 4, 2015, p. 21.

Chapter 4. Getting Ready

1. Kotter, JP. Leading Change: Why Transformation Efforts Fail. Harvard Business Review, March-April, 2000, 59-67.

2. Ibid., p. 60

3. Ibid., p. 64

4. Cloke, K. & Goldsmith, J. End of Management and the Rise of Organizational Democracy. Jossey-Bass, 2002.

Chapter 5. Changing Governance

1. Eichenwald, K. In String of Corporate Troubles, Critics Focus on Boards' Failings. New York Times Online, September, 21, 2003.

2. Sonnenfeld, JA. What Makes Great Boards Great. Harvard Business Review, September, 2002, 106-113.

3. See, e.g., the report, "The Role of the Board of Directors in Enron's Collapse" prepared by the US Senate's Permanent Subcommittee on Investigations, July 28, 2002.

4. Kelly, M. Eureka: An Opening for Economic Democracy. Business Ethics. Summer, 2003, p 4.

5 Byrne, JA. How to Fix Corporate Governance. Business Week, May 4, 2002, 69-78, p.72.

6. See, e.g., Finkelstein, S. & Mooney, AC. Not the Usual Suspects: How to Use Board Process to Make Boards Better. Academy of Management Executive, 2002, Vol. 17, 101-113, p102; Daily, CM., et al. Corporate Governance: Decades of Dialogue and Data. Academy of Management Review, Vol. 28, 2003, 371-382; and Millstein, I. & MacAvoy, P. The Active Board of Directors and Improved Performance of the Large Publicly Traded Company. Columbia Law Review, June, 1998, p1283.

7. Sonnenfeld, op. cit.

8. Morgenson, G. Sticky Scandals, Teflon Directors. The New York Times OnLine, January 29, 2006.

9 See fn. 25.

10. Weil, RL. Board Members Facing Public Scrutiny Should Bone up on Finance and Accounting. Knowledge at Wharton Online, June 18, 2003.

11. Lavelle, L. Enron Directors: Unfit to Serve Anywhere? Business Week Online, February 2, 2002.

12. Zandstra, G. Enron, Board Governance and Moral Failings. Corporate Governance, Vol. 2, 2002, 16-19.

13. Sonnenfeld, op. cit., p.108.

14. Byrne, JA. Commentary: No Excuses for Enron's Board. Business Week Online, July 29, 2002.

Chapter 6. Changing Leadership

1. Byrne, JA. How to Fix Corporate Governance. Business Week, May 4, 2002, 69-78, p72.

2. Byrne, JA., Symonds, WC., & Siler, JF. (1991). CEO Disease: Egotism Can Breed Corporate Disaster. Business Week, (cover story), 52-60.

3. Brumback, GB. Review of The New Psychology of Leadership: Identity, Influence and Power by S. Alexander Haslam, Stephen D. Reicher, & Michael J. Platow. NY: Psychology Press, 2011 in Personnel Psychology, Vol. 68, #1, 2015, pp. 223-227.

4. Thomas, T. et al. Strategic Leadership of Ethical Behavior in Business. Academy of Management Executive, 2004, Vol. 18, 56-66.

5. Churchill, J. 1776. The Key Reporter, Spring, 2006, p. 2

6. Campbell, R. The Industrial-Strength Humanist. The American Scholar, Winter, Vol 74, 2005, 119-121, p. 120.

7. Hill, LA. New Manager Development for the 21st Century. Academy of Management Executive, 2004, Vol. 18, 121-126, p. 125.

8. Morgenson, G. Sticky Scandals, Teflon Directors. The New York Times OnLine, January 29, 2006.

9. Meindl, JR., et al. The Romance of Leadership. Administrative Science Quarterly, Vol. 30, 1985, pp.78-102.

10. Fletcher, JK & Kaufer, K. Shared Leadership. In Pearce, CL. & Conger, JA. Shared Leadership: Reframing the Hows and Whys of Leadership. Sage, 2003.

11. Mulligan, TM. (1987). The Two Cultures in Business Education. Academy of Management Review, Vol. 22, 593-599.

12. Hayes, RH. & Abernathy, W J. Managing Our Way to Economic Decline. Harvard Business Review, Vol. 58, 1980, pp. 67-77

13. Pope, J. MBA Programs Criticized by Stanford Researchers. Associated Press, September 2, 2002.

14. Etzioni, A. Business Schools Fail Ethics. The Washington Post, August 11, 2002.

15. Gladwell, M. The Talent Myth. The New Yorker, July 22, 2002.

16. Surowiecki, J. Good Grooming. The New Yorker, October 4, 2004, p. 40.

17. The Center for Creative Leadership in Greensboro, NC estimated that roughly four billion dollars were spent worldwide in 2003 on leadership development programs. Robert Hogan, who for decades has studied personality and leadership, has estimated that the incidence of managerial incompetence at any one time is around sixty-five to seventy-five percent. See, Hogan, R. Personality and the Fate of Organizations. Erlbaum, 2006.

18. Raelin, JA. Don't Bother Putting Leadership into People. Academy of Management Executive, Vol. 18, 2004, pp. 131-135.

Chapter 7. Changing Board and Leadership Customs

1. Hindo, B. Making the Elephant Dance. Business Week, May 1, 2006, pp. 88-90.

2. See, e.g., Conger, JA. The Dark Side of Leadership, an article reprinted by the American Management Association, 1990; Howell, JM & Avolio, BJ. The Ethics of Charismatic Leadership: Submission or Liberation? Academy of Management Executive, Vol. 6, 1992, pp. 43-54; and Kelly, CM. The Interrelationship of Ethics and Power in Today's Organizations. Organizational Dynamics, Vol. 16, 1987, pp. 5-17.

3. Bebchuk, L. & Fried, J. Pay without Performance: The Unfulfilled Promise of Executive Compensation. Harvard University Press, 2004. See, also, Dalton, DR., et al. Meta-analyses of Financial Performance and Equity: Fusion or Confusion? Academy of Management Journal, Vol. 46, 2003, pp. 13-26.

4. Saha, PM. Novo Nordisk - Sustainable Leadership. Ethical Corporation Online, December 12, 2005.

5. Roner, L. The State of Corporate Citizenship - Words Ahead of the Substance. Ethical Corporation Online, January 17, 2006.

6. Bebchuk & Fried, op. cit. p. 28.

7. Lipton, E. Congressional Charities Pulling In Corporate Cash. The New York Times Online, September 5, 2010. See also, Editorial. Alms for the Rich and Powerful. The New York Times Online, September 7, 2010.

8. Damon, W. The Moral Advantage: How to Succeed in Business by Doing the Right Thing. Berrett-Koehler, 2004.

9. Bennett, RA. High Earnings, Low Ethics. Chief Executive, 2002, pp. 27-29. See also, e.g., Estes, R. Tyranny of the Bottom Line: Why Corporations Make Good People do Bad Things. Berrett-Koehler Publishers, 1996.

10. Useem, M. Investor Capitalism: How Money Managers are Changing the Face of Corporate America. Basic Books, 1996.

11. Byrne, JA. How to Fix Corporate Governance. Business Week, May 4, 2002, pp. 69-78.

12. Brumback, GB. The Devil's Marriage: Break Up the Corpocracy or Leave Democracy in the Lurch. Author House, 2011. See Chapter 10 about ending undemocratic capitalism.

13. Knowledge @ Wharton. Leadership lecture by Xerox CEO Anne Mulcahy at the Wharton School of Business. Knowledge@Wharton Online, November 16-29, 2005.

14. Sorkin, AR. Paper Maker Georgia-Pacific to be Sold to Koch. The New York Times Online, November 14, 2005.

15. Froomkin, D. Starbucks CEO Howard Schultz Calls For Boycott On Campaign Contributions. Huffington Post, August 5, 2011.

16. Nielsen, JS. The Myth of Leadership: Creating Leaderless Organizations. Davies-Black, 2004, p. 95

17. Ireland, RD. & Miller, CC. Decision-making and Firm Success. Academy of Management Executive, Vol. 18, 2004, pp. 8-12.

18. Nutt, PC. Expanding the Search for Alternatives During Strategic Decision-Making. Academy of Management Executive, Vol. 18, 2004, pp. 13-28. See also professor Nutt's book; Why Decisions Fail. Berrett-Koehler, 2002.

19. Bakke, DW. Joy at Work: A Revolutionary Approach to Fun on the Job. Seattle: PVG, 2005.

20. Nutt, op cit.

21. Mitchell, LK. Corporate Irresponsibility: America's Newest Export. Berrett-Koehler, 2001.

22. Nutt, op cit.

Chapter 8. Becoming a Lowerarchy

1. Byrne, JA. The Global Corporation becomes the Leaderless Corporation. Business Week, August 30, 1999, pp. 88-90.

2. See, e.g., Ostroff, F. The Horizontal Organization: What the Organization of the Future Looks Like and How it Delivers Value to Customers. Oxford University Press, 1999.

3. Rodriguez, A. On Matters of Liberation: The Case Against Hierarchy. Hampton Press, 2000.

4. Josephson, M. Holding the Top Man Accountable. Ethics: Easier Said Than Done, Issue 2, 1989, p.26.

5. Richman, LS. When will the Layoffs End? Fortune, September 20, 1993, pp. 54-56.

6. Somerhausen, J. Letter to the Editor, The New Yorker, Jamuary 9, 2004, p. 8.

7. See, e.g., Kidwell, RE. Pink Slips without the Tears. Academy of Management Executive, Vol. 9, 1995, pp. 69-70; Saporito, B. Cutting Costs without Cutting People. Fortune, May 25, 1987, pp. 26-32; and Tomasko, RT. Corporate Streamlining: The Right Way to Shrink a Company. The New York Times Online, January 10, 1988.

8. Hirschhorn, L. & Gilmore, T. The New Boundaries of the "Boundaryless Company. Harvard Business Review, Vol. 70, 1992, pp. 104-115.

9. Brumback, GB. & Vincent, JW. Jobs and Appraisal of Performance. Personnel Administration, Vol. 33, 1970, pp. 26-30.

10. Ostroff, op. cit. p. 131.

11. Ostroff, Ibid.

12. Brumback, GB. Tall Performance from Short Organizations through We/Me Power. Author House, 2002, p. 25. See also; Peters, TJ. & Waterman, RH. Jr. In Search of Excellence. Warner Books, 1982.

13. Specter, M. Rethinking the Brain: How the Songs of Canaries Upset a Fundamental Principle of Science. The New Yorker, April, 2001, pp. 42-53.

14. Maslow, A. Motivation and Personality. Harper, 1954.

15. Rodriguez, op. cit.

16. Peters, T. The Circle of Innovation: You Can't Shrink Your Way to Greatness. Alfred A. Knopf, 1997.

17. Ventura, M. Someone is Stealing Your Life. Utne Reader, July-August, 1991. Reprinted from the L.A. Weekly.

18. See, e.g., Donkin, R. Blood, Sweat, and Tears: The Deterioration of Work. Texere, 2001; Fraser, JA. White-Collar Sweatshop: The Deterioration of Work and its Rewards in Corporate America, 2001; Lawson, K., Savery, J. & Luks, A. The Relationship between Empowerment, Job Satisfaction, and Reported Stress Levels; Some Australian Evidence. Leadership & Organizational Development Journal, Vol. 22, 2001, pp. 97-104; and Ryff,

C. D. Psychological Well Being in Adult Life. Current Directions in Psychological Science, Vol. 4, 1995, pp. 99-104.

19. This is a true quote that I vividly remember. Who could forget it? However, I can't find my reference for it.

20. Robinson E. Toni Morrison's Measured Words. The Washington Post Online, December 8, 1993.

21. Ackroyd, S. & Thompson, P. Organizational Misbehaviour. Thousands Oaks, CA: Sage, 1999.

22. Lawler, E.E. III. Rewarding Excellence: Pay Strategies for the New Economy. San Francisco: Jossey-Bass, 2000.

23. Mans, C. & Sims, H. P. Jr. Business without bosses: How Self-Managing Teams are Building High-Performing Companies. New York, NY: John Wiley & Sons, Inc., 1993.

24. Cloke, K. & Goldsmith, J. End of Management and the Rise of Organizational Democracy. San Francisco, CA: Jossey-Bass, 2002, p4. The arguments for the end of management made by Cloke and Goldsmith are that management turns communication to "one-way streets," sending orders down and preventing unwanted information from heading up; reduces morale and motivation through arrogance, harsh criticism, unresponsiveness, and the like; wastes time waging their career wars up the increasingly narrower promotion ladder; and "constricts quality and service" by discouraging ideas for improvements.

25. Quoted in Tom Peter's book, The Circle of Innovation: You Can't Shrink Your Way to Greatness. NY: Alfred A. Knopf, 1997, p 178.

Chapter 9. Cultivating an Uplifting Culture

1. See, e.g., Bacus, MS. & Near, JP. Can Illegal Behavior be Predicted? An Event History Analysis. Academy of Management Journal, Vol. 34, 1991, pp. 9-36; and Bacus, MS., Near, JP. Schwartz, P & Gibb, B. When Good Companies do Bad Things: Responsibility and Risk in an Age of Globalization. John Wiley & Sons, 1999.

2. Toffler, B. Final Accounting: Ambition, Greed, and the Fall of Arthur Anderson. Broadway Books, 2003

3. Kennedy, AA. The End of Shareholder Value: Corporations at the Crossroads. Cambridge. M.A: Perseus, 2000, pp. 15-17.

4. Josephson, M. Teaching Ethical Decision-Making and Principled Reasoning. Ethics: Easier Said than Done, Issue 1, 1988, pp. 27-33.

5. Step, LS. In Search of Ethics. The Washington Post, March 31, 1991, H1, p. 4.

6. See, e.g., Colquitt, JA. On the Dimensionality of Organizational Justice: A Construct Validation of a Measure. Journal of Applied Psychology, Vol. 86, 2001, pp. 386-400.

7. See, e.g., McGregor, J. Sweet Revenge: The Power of Retribution, Spite, and Loathing in the World of Business. Business Week, January 22, 2007, pp. 64-70.

8. See, e.g., Ciulla, JB. The Working Life: The Promise and Betrayal of Modern Work. Times Books, 2000; Faludi, S. Stiffed: The Betrayal of the Modern Man. William Morrow and Company, 1999; Fraser, JA. White-Collar Sweatshops: The Devaluation of Work and is Rewards in Corporate

America. WW Norton, 2001; and Powell, GN.The Abusive Organization. Academy of Management Executive, Vol. 12, 1998, pp. 95-96.

9. Semler, R. Managing without Managers. Harvard Business Review, Vol. 67, 1989, pp. 76-84, 79.

10. EthicsNewsline. Wal-Mart Searches for Global Ethics Chief: The World's Largest Retailer is Looking for a Top Executive to Bolster its Image, March 3, 2006.

11. 16. Buckley, WF. Jr. "The Defense Bilkers." The Washington Post. August 20, 1985, Op Ed page.

12. Wagel, WH. "A New Focus on Business Ethics at General Dynamics." Personnel, 1987, 64, pp. 4-8.

13. See, e.g., Dwyer, P. & Payne, S. "The General Dynamics Case Sets a Bad Precedent." Business Week, June 8, 1987, p. 41; Lawrence, M. "OSHA Fines Shipbuilder $615,000." The Washington Post, July 30, 1987, E1-2; Ellis, JE & Payne, S. "More Instant Cash than a Lottery: Under GD's Plan, Managers Get a Windfall-and Shareholders Get Ulcers." Business Week, May 20, 1991, p. 42; and Marshall, S. 'After Son's Death, a Pink Slip for Dad', USA Today, March 26, 1993, p. 3A; and Brumback, GB. America's Oldest Professions: Warring and Spying. Create Space, 2015, Chapter 5.

14. Murphy, DE. 10 Year Anniversary Prompts Look at Compliance by Organizations. Web site of the U.S. Sentencing Commission, November 4, 2003.

15. Hyatt, JC. Ethics Officers Double in Four Years. Business Ethics, Spring 2005, p. 9.

See, also, Hyatt, JC. Birth of the Ethics Industry. Business Ethics, Summer 2005, pp. 20-26;

16.. Hyatt, Ibid.; see also, Trevino, LC. & Nelson, KA. Managing Business Ethics: Straight Talk About How To Do It Right. Wiley, 2007 (4th Edition).

17. Hyatt, Ibid; Trevino & Nelson, Ibid.

18. Hyatt, Ibid.

19. Mathews, MC. Strategic Interventions in Organizations: Resolving Ethical Dilemmas. Sage, 1988.

20. Kaye, K. Workplace Wars and How to Avoid Them: Turning Personal Conflicts into
Productive Teamwork. AMACOM, 1994.

21. See, e.g., these other good sources on conflict resolution; Alper, S. et. al. Conflict Management, Efficacy, and Performance in Organizational Teams. Personnel Psychology, Vol. 53, 2000, pp. 625-642; Crawley, J. Constructive Conflict Management: Managing to Make a Difference. Nicholas Bealey Publishing, 1995; and Isenhart, MW. & Spangle, M. Collaborative Approaches to Resolving Conflict. Sage, 2000.

22. See, e.g., Alford, CF. Whistleblowers: Broken Lives and Organizational Power. Cornel University Press, 2001.

23. See, e.g., Miceli, MP & Near, JP. Whistleblowing: Reaping the Benefits. Academy of Management Executive, Vol. 8, 1994, pp. 65-72 for some ideas on how to handle whistle blowing and whistle blowers.

Chapter 10. Managing the Whole Performance

1. See, e.g., Brumback, GB. Tall Performance from Short Organizations through We/Me Power. Author House, 2002.

2. Schiller, B. Stock Price Maximization Drives Corporate Irresponsibility. Ethical Corporation's Europe Conference in London, June 8, 2005. The quotation is of a remark in the conference speech given by Lawrence Mitchell, author of Corporate Irresponsibility: America's Newest Export. Berrett-Koehler, 2001.

3. Dowthat, R., Littlefield, N. & Poe, M. Spoil the CEO. The Atlantic Monthly, May, 2005, p. 52.

4. Punch, M. Dirty Business. Sage, 1996, p. 243.

5. See, e.g., Bacus, MS. & Near, JP. Can Illegal Behavior be Predicted? An Event History Analysis. Academy of Management Journal, 34, 1991, pp.9-36; and Bacus, MS. & Near, JP, Schwartz, P & Gibb, B. When Good Companies do Bad Things: Responsibility and Risk in an Age of Globalization. John Wiley & Sons, 1999.

6. Perl, P. High-tech Methods Boost Productivity, but at a Cost. The Washington Post, September 3, 1984, A28.

7. Hawkins, D. Who's Watching Now? US News and World Report, September 15, pp. 56-57.

8. Eichenwald, K. In String of Corporate Troubles, Critics Focus on Boards' Failings. The New York Times Online, September 25, 2003.

9. Bebchuk, L. & Fried, J. Pay without Performance: The Unfulfilled Promise of Executive Compensation. Harvard University Press, 2004.

10. Brumback, GB. A Performance Appraisal That's Better Than Ratings and Rankings. Workforce Management Online, July 2003, pp. 1-3.

11. Welch, J. & Welch, S. The Case for 20-70-10. Business Week, October 2, 2006, p. 108.

12. The literature is so flush with writings on unconscionable, upside-down rewards and penalties that I hardly know where to begin in giving you some pertinent references. Not that you really need them. You read the news. Nevertheless, what follows with authors in alphabetical order but with no pretense to being representative is a very small sample of references from my bulging files: Corporate Library. New Study Faults High CEO Compensation despite Poor Performance: Report Finds $865 Million in CEO Compensation while Shareholders Suffer $640 Billion in Losses. EthicsOnline, April 10, 2006. (This was a study of eleven companies with high risk ratings). Dash, E. & Leonhardt, D. Insiders Are Selling Like it's 1999. (Not since the early 1970s have executives across America been unloading sizeable portions of their stock, making any attempted link between pay and performance look ludicrous). The New York Times Online, May 23, 2004. Hill, A. Inside Track. Financial Times (London), August 2, 2002, 10 (Executives of the 25 largest companies that went bankrupt from 2001 to 2002 sold nearly three billion dollars of stock just before firms' market value plunged to zero). Kirkland, R. Corporate America's Executive-Compensation System is Broken. Fortune, July 10, 2006, pp. 72-86. (The headline speaks for itself). OMERS. Proxy Voting Guidelines:

Executive Compensation-Golden Parachutes. January 18, 2002, www.Omers.com (Over one-half of 1,500 U.S. companies tracked during one period handed out previously agreed upon severance payments). Saul, S. Study Finds Backdating of Options Widespread. Ethics Newsline, July 17, 2006. (More than 2,000 companies appeared to have used backdated stock options to fatten their top executives' pay packages).

13. Kirkland, Ibid.

14. Drucker, PF. The Practice of Management. Harper & Row, 1954.

15. Bebchuk & Fried, op. cit.

16. See e.g., Alford, CF. Whistleblowers: Broken Lives and Organizational Power. Cornell University Press, 2001; Miceli, MP. & Near, JP. Blowing the Whistle: The Organizational and Legal Implications for Companies and Employees. New York: Lexington Books, 1992; and Miethe, TD. Whistleblowing at Work: Tough Choices in Exposing Fraud, Waste, and Abuse on the Job. Westview Press, 1999.

17. Semler, R. Managing without Managers. Harvard Business Review, Vol. 67, 1989, pp. 76-84, 79.

Chapter 11. Some Alternatives to Corporations

1. Hansen, D. Darwin's Theory of Cooperation. Urban Abundance Project, December 11, 2013.

2. Co-operative News. The Top 300 Cooperatives From Around The World. February 4, 2014.

3. Center for Cooperatives, University of Wisconsin.

4. Ibid.

5. Ibid.

6. Alperovitz, G., Dubb, S. & Howard, T. 7 Cool Companies: The Best Alternatives to Corporate Power. Yes! Magazine, July 29, 2007.

7. National Community Development Association.

8. Lincoln Institute of Land Policy

9. Cutting Edge Capital. The Design of Ownership: The Architecture of Extractive vs. Generative Ownership. January 31, 2012.

10. Wikipedia.

11. Brumback, GB. Tyranny's Hush Money. OpEdNews, September 28, 2013; The Greanville Post, September 29, 2013.

12. Brown, E. Reform of the US Monetary System: Message of 12 Year Old Victoria Grant
Out of the Mouths of Babes: Twelve-Year-Old Money Reformer Tops a Million Views. Global Research, May 20, 2013.

13. Brown, E. Why Public Banks Outperform Private Banks: Unfair Competition or a Better Mousetrap? OpEdNews, February 2, 2015.

14. Schultz, EE. How Employers Raid Pension Plans. The Wall Street Journal, October 2, 2011.

15. Griffith, C. Bad News For State Public Pension Plans. Forbes, November 20, 2014.

Chapter 12. Alternative Capitalism, Not Socialism

1. Korten, D. The Post-Corporate World: Life after Capitalism. Kumerian Press and Berrett-Koehler, 1999, pp. 152-154.

2. Monks, RAG. The New Global Investors: How Shareholders can Unlock Sustainable Prosperity Worldwide. Capstone Publishing Ltd, 2001.

3. Drawn from Appendix C. Brumback, GB. The Devil's Marriage of Leave Corpocracy in the Lurch. Author House, 2011.
4. Barnes, P. Capitalism 3.0: A Guide to Reclaiming the Commons. Berrett-Koehler, 2006, p. 35.

5. Personal communication with Mr. Barnes, February 18, 2010.

6. Barnes, op cit. p. 73.

7. Brumback, op. cit.

8. Eisler, R. The Real Wealth of Nations: Creating a Caring Economics. Berrett-Koehler, 2007, p. 64.

9. Gates, JR. The Ownership Solution: Toward A Shared Capitalism for The 21st Century. Addison-Wesley, 1998.

10. Hawkins, P., Lovins, A., & Lovins, LH. Natural Capitalism: Creating the Next Industrial Revolution. Little Brown & Co., 1999.

11. Terry, R. Economic Insanity: How Growth-Driven Capitalism is Devouring the American Dream. Berrett-Koehler, 1995.

About the Author

Gary Brumback received his undergraduate degree from Indiana University and his Ph.D. in organizational psychology from The Ohio State University in 1963. His doctoral dissertation was on the subject of personal and organizational values.

Retired since 1995, Dr. Brumback had a long and varied career involving the retail industry, the insurance industry, the manufacturing industry, university teaching, the not-for-profit research sector, and the U.S. government.

He was elected a Fellow of both The American Psychological Association and The Association for Psychological Science in recognition of his outstanding and distinguished contributions to psychology. He is also a member of Phi Beta Kappa and Sigma Xi.

He is a prolific writer. His first book, Tall Performance from Short Organizations through We/Me Power is about managing performance in non-hierarchical, empowering organizations. He was invited by the U.S. government to showcase his MBR (managing behavior and results) model of performance management around the country. His book, The Devil's Marriage: Break Up the Corpocracy or Leave Democracy in the Lurch is about the collusion between big corporations and big government to pursue their own self-interests at the expense of the common good. His previous book, America's Oldest Professions: Warring and Spying, gives an unvarnished history of America's foreign and domestic policies and military interventions, explains their causes, describes their consequences, prescribes major reforms, and foretells dismal scenarios of the future if the reforms are not taken.

He has authored over 50 book reviews, many articles in professional journals, and many technical reports. He has given many talks at professional meetings in the U.S. and abroad. His invited addresses on serious matters have always added a touch of humor. He dressed as "Capt. No No," for example, in his talk on an oxymoron, "government ethics." His research, writings, and presentations have covered a broad array of topics.

Since retiring he has gone beyond his own field to delve into economics, history, humanism, moral philosophy, political science, public affairs, and theology. He researched all of those subjects to help him write The Devil's Marriage: Break Up the Corpocracy or Leave Democracy in the Lurch, America's Oldest Professions: Warring and Spying, and the present book.

www.ingramcontent.com/pod-product-compliance
Lightning Source LLC
Chambersburg PA
CBHW051909170526
45168CB00001B/306